D0463052

the reluctant entertainer

every woman's
guide to simple
and gracious hospitality

the reluctant entertainer

every woman's
guide to simple
and gracious hospitality

SANDY COUGHLIN

BETHANY HOUSE PUBLISHERS
Minneapolis, Minnesota

Published by Bethany House Publishers
11400 Hampshire Avenue South
Bloomington, Minnesota 55438

Bethany House Publishers is a division of
Baker Publishing Group, Grand Rapids, Michigan.

Printed in China

Library of Congress Cataloging-in-Publication Data

Coughlin, Sandy.
  The reluctant entertainer : every woman's guide to simple and gracious hospitality / Sandy Coughlin.
    p. cm.
  Summary: "Experienced hostess and popular blogger gives reluctant entertainers encouragement and advice for successful hospitality without fear. Includes practical tips, techniques, recipes, and advice"—Provided by publisher.
  ISBN 978-0-7642-0750-1 (alk. paper)
  1. Entertaining. 2. Cookery. I. Title.
  TX731.C675 2010
  642'.4—dc22

                                                                                2010006324

Beyond words, my mother, Millie, gave me the foundation for living a hospitable life. From the day I was born, she taught me about love, hospitality, and people. The night she left this world has forever left a hole in my heart.

Auntie Ellen was my Balcony Girl in life, encouraging and cheering me on. She taught me about creativity, how to make people feel special, and the importance of making memories. Your red lipstick made a statement, Auntie Ellen, just as your life was a bright inspiration!

Sandy Coughlin is creator of the popular blog Reluctant Entertainer, which she began in 2006 to help women get past their entertaining fears. Sandy has appeared on nationally broadcast television and radio programs, is a frequent contributor to Crosswalk.com, and has blogged for SCJohnson .com, AWomanInspiredConference.com, Kyria.com, and other online publications. A busy mom of three teenagers, Sandy is active in various volunteer organizations, and she enjoys ballroom dancing, hosting parties, cooking, and running. Sandy is married to Paul, and the family practices hospitality in their hometown of Medford, Oregon.

Visit Sandy's blog at ReluctantEntertainer.com.

CONTENTS

Real Entertaining for Real People

Okay, ladies, let's have a show of hands. Everyone who feels like they just don't have what it takes to pull off a successful meal or a party in your home, raise your hand. I see your nervous hands! Now, everyone who feels totally at ease and 100 percent sure of yourself as a hostess, raise your confident hand.... Um, where did the hands go?

I know the reasons why those hands stay stuck to our sides. I also know the simple steps necessary to fix this growing problem that keeps us and our families isolated instead of connected—alone instead of together. Through my blog, Reluctant Entertainer, I have helped women across the country transform from a reluctant entertainer to a confident one.

One of the main reasons we remain reluctant and isolated is that we have bought in to the thinking that perfection is required in order to be hospitable. This belief is a mistake I once held, which I realized after eating dinner at a friend's house.

As a young mother with a baby on the way, I was apprehensive when my husband, Paul, came home from work and informed me that we were going to the home of a new artist friend of Paul's for dinner. Because I didn't know the family, I felt nervous. But as

I walked into their home, I realized it was . . . normal. It actually was a little chaotic, as four small children ran around in the usual sequence of life.

My senses kicked into high gear as I smelled the incredible aroma of garlic and fresh bread. Right away I felt at home. We sat down to a feast of some of the best Italian cooking I've ever tasted. The hostess was gorgeous inside and out. Her dark Italian eyes were piercing, and her smile welcoming. Her hair was long and mussed up, and I don't even remember her clothing, but I do remember the glow about her as she served us.

I realized later that our conversation was different from what I had experienced at many social events. It was real. I thought, *These people are not trying to impress.* They truly cared about us, about our family and our lives. Even though their home seemed slightly out of order, they knew the true meaning of hospitality: It's a matter of the heart. They understood people and connection. They took these essential ingredients of hospitality and put them to use. They understood that hospitality is unique to rebuilding communities, restoring relationships, and reviving families.

GLUE THAT CONNECTS

What a lesson for me. Little did I know how that meal would shape my thinking and help me become more flexible. As I watched the dynamics of this home and the love that flowed—while kids ran everywhere and dishes stacked up by the sink—I realized hospitality doesn't have to be perfect, it just needs to be from the heart. It's the glue that connects us with each other.

I love to share this story to point out that hospitality comes in different shapes and sizes. To some it may mean an elaborate dinner party. To others it's a casual party with kids underfoot. And to some others it may mean opening their home to out-of-town company or taking cookies to a neighbor. Understanding people is an art in itself, and it's a big piece of the pie when it comes to simple acts of kindness that you can offer to anyone.

When I think about the core of hospitality, I think of this statement from Chuck Swindoll's book *Dropping Your Guard*:

> *It is only when I share life's experiences with others that I can enjoy them or endure them to the greatest advantage. You see, having a relationship calls for being in fellowship with others, and that cannot be done very easily at arm's length. It implies getting in touch, feeling the hurts, being an instrument of encouragement and healing. Fences must come down. Masks need to come off.* Welcome signs need to be hung outside the door. *Keys to the locks in our lives must be duplicated and distributed. Bridges need to be lowered that allow others to cross the moat and then share our joys and our sorrows.* (emphasis added)

Paul and I have experienced hospitality many times around our table. We are always amazed at how God works through food, conversation, authenticity, and laughter. Hospitality is not just a potluck dish. It's about relating to people on a deeper level in a way that reflects your life and style while forming stronger bonds. Hospitality happens over real meals that are cooked by real people, and draws people from the cold world of isolation and into the warmth of connection and friendship. I know because it happens in our home over and over.

So when did we determine that entertaining requires perfection? Is that really what hospitality is all about?

Don't let pie-in-the-sky perfectionism haunt you! Instead of allowing the food, the table setting, and your home to be the focus of your entertaining, put your guests first. Your surroundings will become less significant. You'll experience greater community, deeper friendships, and a wider support structure. You'll benefit from the realization that the joy of giving is much stronger than the joy of receiving. And it's not as hard as you might think.

You will no longer say, "Hospitality just isn't my gift." You will be enthused as you discover that gracious living is the butter on the warm bread of common life.

HOSPITALITY ROOTS

I was fortunate growing up, because my mother passed on to me the gift of loving people through hospitality. And her love for people came from her mom, my Grandma Dubs. When I was a little girl, my grandma told me stories of feeding the hungry during the Great Depression.

Grandma and Grandpa owned a trailer park where they willingly shared food with strangers who would come and go. They'd also share a strong cup of coffee and a bit of encouragement from Grandma's deep Christian faith, then send them on their way. Reaching out to strangers came easily to Grandma because she had promised herself she would be good to others and wise with what she was given. Both sets of my grandparents were great examples of being hospitable people, and my parents reaped the blessings.

My mom, Millie, passed down the torch of loving others as she started her own family and practiced hospitality along with my dad. Mom didn't get caught up in over-commitments or in impressing others with over-the-top entertaining. She didn't rely on television shows or magazines to improve her entertaining skills. Her simple china, a Betty Crocker cookbook, a couple of aprons, and some linens for the table were just about all she needed. Mom knew what reaching out to others was about: simplicity and love.

When Mom passed away thirteen years ago, she was remembered for her love for people and reaching out. The art of hospitality was just a way of life for her.

For some women, hospitality is very natural. For others, it takes work and effort. But for all of us, it must be cultivated so that it can become a channel for amazing experiences. It's exciting when you can step outside of your fears and into the realm of putting others first.

Eleanor Roosevelt put it this way: "You gain strength, courage, and confidence by every experience in which you really stop to look fear in the face. . . . You must do the thing you think you cannot do."

Hospitality seems to have skipped a generation, or even two. It just seems different today. Through teaching my children and sharing simple hospitality insights with women across the country, I find we have a deep

It's been proven that hospitality benefits us in the long run because we will have healthier and longer lives than those who are lonely.

Strawberry Salad

This recipe came from my sweet niece Addie. It's also delicious with raspberries. Serves 8 to 10.

Salad:
- 10 oz. spring-mix greens
- ½ lb. cooked bacon, crumbled
- 1 pint fresh strawberries, sliced
- ½ cup slivered almonds, toasted
- 1 pkg. ramen noodles, toasted
- ¼ cup sesame seeds, toasted

Dressing:
- ½ cup oil
- ¼ cup sugar
- 2 T. white wine vinegar
- ½ tsp. pepper
- ½ tsp. salt

Toss greens, bacon, strawberries, almonds, noodles, and sesame seeds together. Set aside. Combine oil, sugar, vinegar, pepper, and salt and mix well. Dress the salad just before serving.

Tip: Toast the almonds, noodles, and seeds separately in the oven. If you don't want to heat your oven, here's a quicker way: Place item to be toasted on a paper towel and microwave 1 minute. Stir. Microwave for additional minute or until browned.

yearning to discover what has been lost and a strong desire to bring it back. We live in a different generation now, and the difference lies in the fact that there's more "permission" today to not have it all together.

We're more free to be who we are, without the pressures for perfection. At the same time, many of us feel we're not gifted in homemaking, but we are longing and willing to try to learn about this missing element in our lives. We want to reach out, but our busy schedules, perfectionism, fear of criticism, and just not knowing how stop us.

I am not a chef, but what does bring me pleasure is cooking for others. I really enjoy inspiring small-group parties where connection is made.

During our parties, things are never perfect. Mishaps happen, but my focus always remains the same: getting to know others in ways that I didn't know before.

CATCH THE SPARK

I believe that times are changing. The desire to resurrect the lost art of hospitality is growing, bringing people back to their roots and realizing what is missing in their lives: fellowship.

It could be as simple as this. My friend Kay shared with me how one of her neighbors lost his job. The family was reeling from several devastating months of no work, yet in uncertain times, she'd find them out in their yard, right next to the street, barbecuing with friends around them.

Out of a hospitable spirit, we can show others that they are loved.

Kay said they would always wave and say hello and invite Kay and her husband over. They'd extend a good amount of friendliness. My point: It takes effort to smile, to be thankful, and to keep a positive attitude even when times get rough.

In fact, the hard times are often when we need each other the most.

Hospitality starts with a desire. Then, by catching the spark through the promise of guidance in this book, you'll find it won't be as hard as you think.

Simple entertaining combined with some inspiration can create spiritual monuments in our lives. It not only gives us hope, but it teaches us the benefits of moving forward and not looking back. It is a beautiful gift without a price tag.

Find the insights in this book that are the simplest to implement, those that grab your passion the most, and then run with them. You'll find you'll have the energy to reach out when you're doing something that has meaning and fits who you are.

You'll be able to raise your hand in confidence, pass the gift down to your family members, and become a good role model to your friends.

So leave your nervousness and reluctance behind and journey with me through *The Reluctant Entertainer* as I paint for you how easy and gracious entertaining can be.

Grasp a ray of hope, catch the spark, and let's begin by living graciously.

Easy Sweet Potatoes

These can be prepared a day or two ahead of time. In our home we say sweet potatoes are like candy. Kids love them! Serves 8.

8 medium sweet potatoes
¼ cup cream (whipping or
   half-and-half)
¼ cup brown sugar
¼ cup melted butter

1 tsp. ground cinnamon
1 tsp. salt
½ cup fresh orange juice
3 T. grated orange rind (optional)

Preheat oven to 350°F. Place potatoes on a foil-lined cookie sheet, and bake for approximately 1 hour (depending on size) or until soft.

Remove the potatoes from oven and let cool. Once potatoes are cool, peel them and put them in a bowl with remaining ingredients. Beat with a hand mixer. Heat in the microwave just before serving.

Variation: Prepare ingredients as above. Preheat oven to 375°F. Beat 2 eggs into the mixture, whipping on high speed until fluffy. Pour into a 9" x 13" baking pan sprayed with nonstick cooking spray. Combine ⅓ cup brown sugar, ¼ cup shredded coconut, ¼ cup flour, and ¼ cup melted butter and spread over the top. Bake for 20 to 25 minutes.

Joy Busters and Joy Building

My heart aches when people suffer simply because they are searching for something to take their loneliness away. I've read the heartfelt comments on my blog from women sharing their fears, inabilities, and concerns about entertaining. While their desire to be hospitable is real, so are their dissatisfaction and their fears. One woman was afraid to invite people into her home because she feared their possible rejection. Another confessed that she was intimidated by conversation. Many were honest about their perfectionist upbringings, while others had visions of perfection bouncing around in their heads thanks to unrealistic media.

Instead of embracing hospitality, they spend their time making excuses or engaging in dangerous wishful thinking: "I wish I had a bigger house," "I wish I were married," "I wish my children would grow up," "I wish I had more money," "I wish I had the time," "I wish I were more creative," "I wish I could entertain like her," and so on.

I call these negative thoughts *joy busters*. They stop us from seeing joyful entertaining and meaningful hospitality clearly, consequently harming our souls and community.

The great writer and thinker Henri Nouwen has challenged, inspired, and taught me to trust God in a more profound way when

it comes to the deeper meaning of entertaining and hospitality. Nouwen throws a fresh light on hospitality by reminding us of our mortality and our brokenness, and of how in our hurts and loneliness we can experience healing through true hospitality—when we become open and real with one another. He reminds us that hospitality can convert our woundedness into a source of healing. But to reach such healing, we have to confront our insecurities with courage, gentleness, and grace.

He writes in *The Wounded Healer*, "False hope leads us to make exhausting demands and prepares us for bitterness and dangerous hostility when we start discovering that nobody, and nothing, can live up to our absolutistic expectations." When we read this, we usually think about the exhausting demands put upon our guests, but it also includes our own families. Many children, as they grow up, learn to fear entertaining instead of embrace it.

Joy busters are the irrational fears we let sneak into our minds, the fears that destroy the joys we could be reveling in—joys such as connection, laughter, and deeper friendships that could actually enhance our lives.

A friend recently shared about her decision to let go of perfection. All too aware of some wealthy friends who ran in her circle, she always felt intimidated to even try to have a dinner party. Finally she decided to rid herself of those lies that were bogging her down: fanciness; perfection; material stuff like her home, yard, and dishes; and even how her kids were supposed to act. But eventually, as she practiced hospitality, it actually made her more joyful. She began to feel more at home in her home and at ease with herself in a way she'd never felt before. As we discussed this newfound freedom she'd busted through to, she and I both got teary sharing the beauty of providing an open and fearless place for others to come and rest.

Initiating and practicing hospitality sometimes means doing some soul searching. It does take effort to go deeper into the lives of our neighbors or someone at church who's having surgery or a family who just lost a loved one. Writes Nouwen, "Anyone who wants to pay attention without intention has to be at home in his own house—that is, he has to discover the center of his life in his own heart." This tells me that you don't even have to have a home to make someone feel warm and welcome. I call this *taking your hospitality with you*, an idea that we'll explore more in chapter 8. We check our hearts, we open them up to others, and we take our hospitable spirit with us.

That effort recently became reality to me as I was driving through my old neighborhood and stopped to visit a neighbor of ten years who had just lost her husband. I felt the pull of my steering wheel and I knew I needed to stop in for a quick visit. But my joyous visit with Jean was almost squelched by my initial thought, *I don't have anything to bring her!* She is just one of those classy ladies whom you'd want to bring a small token of love to.

Put the lies to rest. Realize that a successful time of entertaining is measured by the way your guests feel when they leave your home.

It's crazy that we think we always have to do something or bring something or say something. But this day, as I found myself with no material gift, I didn't realize until I drove off that my ability to listen to and encourage my lonely friend was probably the best gift I could give. I was reminded of Nouwen's words, "We can only love because we are born out of love, that we can only give because our life is a gift, and that we can only make others free because we are set free by Him whose heart is greater than ours."

Let's take a look at some of the most common joy busters and how you can overcome them.

JOY BUSTERS

WHOM TO INVITE

Some people don't practice hospitality because they fear rejection. Some don't have any friends they'd want to have over—or they have too many friends and find it hard to choose whom to invite. I find it interesting that very few people talk about inviting "new" friends over. I know what this is like. During the busiest season of life right now with three teens, I find it's not always easy to forge new relationships.

My husband and I were invited to a young couple's home last summer. We had never met them before. They knew who we were through mutual friends, from our Web sites, and from Paul's writing and speaking. We connected through email, set a date, and joined this couple from New Zealand for dinner. We were glad to take the invitation, but initially we were a little uncomfortable.

Today Fiona, the brave hostess who reached out to us through the Internet, has become one of my dearest friends and greatest gifts in life. If I had said no to this new friendship, I would have lost out. I'm sure this dinner invite was risky for them too. Though they had heard about us and were familiar with our somewhat public lives, they didn't know

us. But I'm glad the four of us trusted one another and were willing to forge something new. And we were blessed.

I DON'T KNOW HOW TO COOK.

For women who are intimidated by the meal part of cooking, a get-together is the big scare. It's not that they don't know how to cook—almost everyone knows how to cook something. The real issue is that they don't cook as well as they would like to cook. It's important to remember that we are all on a spectrum when it comes to cooking. And we all have the capacity to improve. So instead of saying you don't know how to cook, tell yourself, "I would like to learn how to cook a little better than I currently do." This better attitude has so much more hope and optimism attached to it.

Last year as I was coming home from a trip, I met a young mommy in the airport. She had her new baby with her, and she was so exhausted from layovers and getting bumped that she had no problem opening up and sharing with me. I like to get to know people and I love babies, so I asked her what role hospitality plays in her life. She looked at me, shocked, and said, "My mom never taught me how to cook." Her mom did everything for her and her sisters growing up, including cooking. So when she got married, she was stuck. She told me that she longs to have people in her home so she can get to know them and they can get to know her. But she has bought in to the joy buster that she doesn't know how to prepare even a simple meal and can't envision ever changing this situation in her life.

So maybe you don't know how to cook as well as you'd like, or maybe you're just uninterested in cooking. That's okay, because when it comes to hospitality, you can always order takeout, buy a pizza, or even take a class. Your lack of culinary skills shouldn't stop you from reaping the blessings of inviting people into your life.

As you will discover, hospitality and learning more about food take effort. When I first started entertaining, I prepared the same three dishes over and over again until I eventually memorized the recipes. The more I cooked, the more efficient I became. It is often said that practice makes perfect. I don't really think that is true. Practice does, however, make things better—and that's good enough. So when you practice the same recipe over and over, think in terms of excellence, not that joy buster perfection.

MY FOOD NEVER TURNS OUT

Two summers ago we had friends over for dinner. When one of my guests asked if she could contribute, I willingly agreed that she should bring some pies. Homemade, store-bought, Grandma's pie—I didn't care who made them or what they looked like. Everyone loves a pie!

When all the guests arrived, I was surprised to see that she had a completely different dessert in her hands. This was fine with me, because I often deviate from my original plan. I've learned to go with the flow.

But we learned later that she had ever so slightly burned her pies and tossed them into the garbage. All the time spent on making something perfect turned to disaster for her. Our family would simply have added ice cream if a dessert was a bit toasty, and we would have devoured the pie anyway. Once again, perfection became a joy buster.

MY HOUSE ISN'T UP TO PAR

"My house isn't clean enough" was one of the most popular cries from women confessing their greatest challenge when I asked on my blog, "What stops you from entertaining?" It was this complaint, along with a concern that they didn't have adequate space or seating for their guests, that caused the most reluctance in my readers.

They also felt like they were not organized enough to have people over—they didn't quite have it together in preparation, and the nitty-gritty details often bogged them down. The insecurities of not keeping a perfect home and fears of rejection from others were huge factors.

My mother's childhood friend Vinnie has lived a life of hospitality. She shared with me her struggles in her younger days. She finally came

Bacon Chestnuts

My friend Jenny brought these to our house for a New Year's Eve party years ago. Since then, they've become a favorite. Serves 6 to 8.

1 pound thick-cut bacon,
    cut in thirds
2 (8 oz.) cans whole
    water chestnuts, drained
½ cup soy sauce
¼ cup packed brown sugar
¼ tsp. ground ginger
2 cloves crushed garlic

Mix soy sauce, brown sugar, ginger, and garlic together. Marinate the water chestnuts in this sauce in the refrigerator for 2 hours.

Preheat oven to 350°F. Drain the marinade. Wrap each water chestnut in a third slice of bacon and secure with a toothpick. Place on a foil-lined pan. Bake 20–25 minutes, until crisp. Serve warm.

Optional dipping sauce: Mix together ¼ cup barbecue sauce, ¼ cup mayonnaise, and 2 T. brown sugar.

Variation: Instead of water chestnuts, wrap bacon around almonds, dates, or cubes of precooked chicken.

to the realization that in order to overcome the nagging worries about her house being clean, she had to just let go and focus on her guests and a quick, easy meal. Those two aspects freed her in the upcoming years to reach out to others.

I decided long ago that I'd much rather bake and share cookies with my neighbor than run around making a perfect house. I'd rather let my kids help in the kitchen, lick the spoons, and often make a mess than say no to getting them involved. I let go of the fear of messes and embraced my kids and the other people around me.

I'M JUST TOO BUSY

Our world seems to get more and more impersonal, everyone rushing around, crazily living their lives—my family included. I've heard from several moms, new to their city, feeling it's just too hard to "connect." People seem to have their inner circle locked in, as if there isn't room for more. That is very sad.

Our neighborhoods are packed with families, yet we are lonely and so uninvolved in each other's lives. Garage doors are opening and shutting several times a day without even a hello, and connection is the missing key. I watch it in my neighborhood, and even though we know this truth, we are still guilty. I've started questioning and asking myself if my life is full of meaningful accomplishments or just busy activities. It's sometimes hard to evaluate our motives. So in order to get to the soul of entertaining and hospitality, I find this proverb from Nouwen extremely helpful: "Hospitality asks for the creation of an empty space where the guest can find his own soul."

WE CAN'T AFFORD IT

Giving up the idea that we women have to do it all, which can include a pretty high price tag, I am reminded that a simple get-together can be potluck: a time to delegate dishes and allow friends to contribute. The cost of food is so expensive these days that I don't see how we can afford not to ask our guests to help out sometimes. So we have to put our pride away and stop thinking we have to do it all.

I've hunkered down this last year, trying to keep the menu within my price range and letting my guests participate in the meal. It's taken the pressure off my time and my pocketbook and has allowed me to continue to entertain.

IT'S TOO HARD WITH KIDS

If we could put away the image of perfect dinner parties, then we wouldn't be so hard on ourselves when it comes time to entertain with kids. Parents overcomplicate the matter, thinking they have to cook a special meal for the little ones, or they worry about kids running wildly through their home, messing it up. Now, I know it's not okay to trash people's homes, and that boundaries and limits should be set, but I also don't agree with isolating kids to a corner of the house.

Entertaining kids can be as simple as making up a box of mac and cheese, cutting up a bowl of fruit, or letting them munch on the adults' bread. My goal has always been to feed the kids first and then let them play or watch a movie and have their own fun while adults enjoy adult time. I found that getting the kids' routine down and doing the same thing every time helped me put energy into cooking the adult meal. The bottom line is kids don't care; they just want to have fun.

I CAN'T DO IT ALONE

Being a solo hostess isn't always easy. Whether you're divorced, widowed, never married, or married to someone who travels frequently, it can be scary entertaining alone. But if you keep it simple and have a plan, a gathering really can come together when you have only two hands to do all the work. I think of my friend Jenny, who in her single years was very good at having couples over. In order to lift the load, she would ask each guest to bring a part of the menu, and when we'd arrive at her home, she'd grab one of the guys and ask him to BBQ—something you don't have to ask a man twice to do. These get-togethers helped Jenny make it through a challenging time in her life, and they gave us, her friends, another opportunity to be there with her and for her.

One of my cousins told me recently, "When the kids were younger and I was married, I loved to entertain. After my divorce I think that part of me disappeared, because hospitality had been such a family affair and we all participated. And our friends kind of disappeared after we divorced. Divorce is such a rotten part of society and families. I never thought it would be part of my life."

Being single when you don't want to be single is tough. I remember those years, especially the loneliness that at times felt unbearable. This is when I think being hospitable can be its most helpful to you and others. This is when we need to spend more time with family and friends in order to ward off the harm that comes from too much time alone.

MY HUSBAND ISN'T INTERESTED IN ENTERTAINING

If there's one thing my blog has told me, it's that wives want to entertain more than husbands do. Men are social beings, but not in the way most women are. In fact, our ideas of entertaining were a source of contention between my husband and me when we were newly married. (The rub had to do with conversation. See chapter 7.) My view is that the guy wants things simple: good food, easy conversation, and relaxation. We women sometimes mess that up because we make things too complicated, due in part to some unhealthy expectations forced upon us by the media. We all look up to Martha Stewart, who makes it look so easy.

A while back I was asked to speak about hospitality to a ladies group at my friend's home. What I shared about hospitality was very simple. I encouraged these young moms to find healthy mentors, to foster friendships with like-minded women, and to explore their passions in sharing the civic and common life together. But I wanted to point out the one simple ingredient to healthy hospitality that we women sometimes forget: It is essential to love your spouse. That love should be like a garment that we constantly wear and never remove. I shared a painful story from early on in my marriage when I loved entertaining more than my husband did. I was too pushy with what I wanted, with what I was trying to accomplish (plan the perfect meal, set the perfect table, etc.), and it caused strains in my marriage. It took me a few years to discover what true hospitality was all about and to forge a new path for my husband and me, a path we both enjoy today.

Another helpful step is to evaluate your stress level and see if you're adding tension to those around you, possibly bursting their joy completely. Try to get ready an hour before company arrives so you can sit down and relax for a bit. This will help you be in the right frame of mind when company arrives.

JOY-BUILDING TEN COMMANDMENTS

Now that I've shared with you the main joy busters that stop us from living a more hospitable life, I'm happy to share with you a simple list of "hospitality rules" that I came up with when I started my blog years ago. I originally wrote this list for me. It still keeps me grounded in what hospitality is all about, helps me push past fears, and basically gives me a pep talk that says, "I can do this!" My ten commandments have been effective across the country, as ladies have asked to hang them on their refrigerators and Mothers of Preschoolers (MOPS) groups have shared them at their monthly meetings. Women shared with me that having a plan, and a list of boundaries to encourage them in hospitality, gave them freedom, hope, and inspiration.

MY TEN COMMANDMENTS OF HOSPITALITY

COMMANDMENT 1
Hospitality is not about you.
It's about making others feel warm and welcome.

COMMANDMENT 2
Plan ahead, be organized, and know your recipe. Learn to delegate.

COMMANDMENT 3
Set the mood. Keep ambience and the five senses in mind.

COMMANDMENT 4
Avoid perfectionism. Put fear aside—it's a robber of anything good.

COMMANDMENT 5
Share conversation. Foster friendships by keeping things real.

COMMANDMENT 6
Demonstrate thriftiness. Buying things at cost or learning to pinch
pennies makes entertaining attainable on a budget.

COMMANDMENT 7
Don't apologize. It's okay to make mistakes. Learn to not bring them
to light in front of your guests; it robs your guests of relaxation.

COMMANDMENT 8
Be creative. Use what you have. Keep things simple.

COMMANDMENT 9
Learn from others. Find mentors and learn to find a healthy balance
and keep things real.

COMMANDMENT 10
Life impact is everything. Experience intimacy and meaning
in sharing a meal and gleaning from others' lives.

NO MORE BUSTERS

I think of my friend Jami, who is a very busy mom of fourteen-year-old quadruplets. She has a unique approach toward hospitality. Although she says she is hospitality-challenged, I disagree. She says that she didn't learn hospitable traits growing up, so everything she does she has learned from watching others. I'd say Jami has pushed past the joy busters in her life and on to a better way of living.

Early on, Jami's idea of entertaining was opening a can of soup or ordering a few large pizzas. Now she has a couple of large gatherings a year, inviting up to forty people, instead of entertaining more times throughout the year. I asked Jami to share with me what helped her decide to open up her home. "What helped me was going outside my comfort zone, facing my fears, and actually doing things I didn't think I could do. I also like to do things that will force me to trust God more and rely on Him to make things how they should be. I've learned to give up control and to remember that life is about people, loving them sincerely, and forgetting about trying to impress!" Jami's "get it done all at once" approach of hosting a large gathering is definitely inspiring.

So with the insights in this chapter, you are now well on your way to do more than dream. You now have ideas for how to turn your dreams into reality. But one thing may be stopping you. If you're like most people who long to transform from a reluctant to a gracious entertainer, the one thing you might be missing is courage and the strength that comes from courage. One of the best ways to grow courage is experiencing success, so my advice to you is KISS: Keep It Simple, Sister. Start small and take it from there. Pick one or two of my ten commandments of hospitality that are most relevant to your life, and implement them today. With time and the inspiration found here, you will find yourself growing and helping others in ways you wouldn't have imagined when you began this heartfelt journey. There is a desire within each of us to grow in hospitality. And the reason for this is deeper than we might see at first.

I do not think there is anyone who understands hospitality's deeper meaning and spiritual significance more than Nouwen. I'd like to share one final piece of wisdom from him:

Hospitality is the virtue which allows us to break through the narrowness of our own fears and to open houses to the stranger, with the intuition that salvation comes to us in the form of a tired traveler. Hospitality makes anxious disciples into powerful witnesses, makes suspicious owners into generous givers, and makes closed-minded sectarians into interested recipients of new ideas and insights.

Like a person learning to swim, the best way to make it to the deep water that Nouwen describes is by starting at the shallow end. After a few successes, along with a setback or two, the water at both ends will feel pretty much the same.

Watermelon Summer Salad

The first time I had this salad was in Chicago while visiting the Kraft Foods Kitchen. Mouthwatering goodness! Serves 6.

¾ cup halved, thinly sliced red onion
1 T. fresh lime juice
1½ quarts seeded, cubed watermelon
¾ cup crumbled feta cheese
½ cup pitted black olives, sliced in half
1 cup chopped fresh mint
2 T. olive oil

Marinate the onion slices in the lime juice for 10 minutes.

In a large bowl, toss together the watermelon, feta, olives, mint, onions with the lime juice, and olive oil.

Overcoming the Pitfalls of Perfectionism

In my earlier years of entertaining, I'd try to live up to perfect standards—you know, like having a perfectly cooked meal and a home that wasn't just clean and presentable but perfect and immaculate. But when I didn't meet those perfectionist standards and things fell apart, I'd be downright miserable, often bringing others down with me.

Like when I slightly overcooked my piecrust and didn't have time to make another one, or the bathroom counters weren't perfectly clean, or the kids weren't cooperating with my schedule, causing me to be a mean and grumpy mom—my whole family would suffer right alongside me. My internal misery became their misery as well, and that was a real shame.

It was around this time that my husband shared this insight into the problem of perfectionism, and it changed the way I approached hospitality. He told me, "Perfectionism is a jail cell locked from inside, creating your own misery." He explained that there is a huge difference between trying to be excellent at what you do and trying to be perfect at something. Excellence is working toward an attainable goal that benefits everyone, while perfection comes

three

from a place of great need—usually the need to avoid criticism and gain praise and approval from others. I brought these insights into blogland and found they helped liberate thousands of women from the jail cell of perfectionism.

Get out of the jail cell of perfectionism by asking yourself, "Am I having people in to my home to impress them or to bless them?"

When it comes to hospitality, the fact is, perfectionism is downright selfish. It's cruel to you and others. It undercuts your efforts to create true hospitality, which has more to do with creating the right mood than the perfect piecrust.

Defeating the cruel voice of perfectionism takes time. Like most women, I still struggle with it from time to time. For example, last summer we had out-of-town guests, and my daughter agreed to make her favorite—banana cream pie (see recipe on page 151). When I saw the finished product, I kept myself from saying to her, "Abby, you forgot to soak the bananas in lemon juice! And you didn't put them on the bottom of the pie, where they wouldn't turn brown!"

Instead I said . . . nothing. I almost walked back into that jail cell and locked my daughter in there with me. Abby's pie tasted no different with brown bananas. The flavor was a hit at our dinner party, and the pie was topped with real whipped cream anyway, so our guests didn't even see the brown bananas.

As I continue to give the perfectionist jailer the boot in my mind, I'm opening the door for Abby to go where her passion and interests lead her, bringing both of us a lot of joy.

FIRST IMPRESSIONS

First impressions are important when it comes to entertaining, but what really draws people together is genuine love and authenticity. One definition of authenticity that gets to the heart of real hospitality is this: "Relating to or denoting an emotionally appropriate, significant, purposeful, and responsible mode

of human life." I love this definition because it shows just how important being authentic is to relationships. Authenticity is honest and doesn't try to needlessly impress others. And the great thing about being authentic is that it attracts other authentic people—those who are soulful and who make the greatest friends.

One hot summer night, my friend Selena and her family stopped in for a visit. I had met Selena through my blog, and when I learned they would be traveling through Oregon, we invited them to stop in for some cold drinks, strawberry pie, and a quick dip in the pool for their kids. It was an opportunity to share and be real with these people. Our home was not at all perfect that night, and in fact I remember our family being very busy that day, so when they arrived I wanted to quickly usher them to the backyard. A few weeks after their visit, we heard from Selena about her family's three-week house swap in a modern 1970s California home. She noted how, as "cool and modern" as this home they were staying in was, it was rather cold and sterile. She said, "This house may rock, but it certainly doesn't have much soul. Your house dripped of soul and kindness." Those words have stuck in my head. When we meet strangers and show hospitality, how do we come across to them? What are the first impressions? And does our home drip with soul and kindness?

Imagine walking into a beautiful home with an elaborate table setting and an incredible aroma coming from the kitchen. You'll probably initially be impressed, thinking a great experience is ahead. Who doesn't love beauty and gourmet cooking? But then, once you meet the host and hostess and find they are phony, off-putting, and even insulting, your opinion probably changes drastically from your first impression. This is because the night would be about impression and not about purpose.

Being a hospitable hostess means loving, giving, and making others feel warm and welcomed. It's not about stuff, glamor, or glitz. It's about fostering authentic relationships.

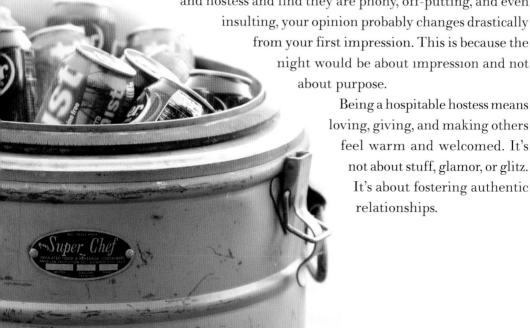

So first impressions are important, but important in a way that we aren't very used to hearing. When we invite people into our homes, we want that greeting and the experience to be a good one. It's about being real, warm, and authentic—purpose over impression.

PERFECTIONISM'S MOUTHPIECE: THE MEDIA

Television shows, magazines, Web sites, and more inundate us with entertaining ideas that, on the surface, seem to bring us enjoyment. But often, after a while, they actually bring us pain, especially during a down economy. It is from the media that I received my infection of perfectionism even though I grew up in a home that modeled genuine hospitality. And I thought, *If I, who had a mom who showed me authentic hospitality, can be sucked into the jail cell of perfectionism, escape from it must be even harder for those women whose mothers didn't model hospitality.*

Like many women, I began my adventure in entertaining during my early twenties—a time when I didn't think as much about how I was treating others. Then while in my thirties I was more about impressing others by being able to do it all—you know, clean the house and cook the entire meal without asking for any help from anyone. Then in my forties I finally learned to not be so worried about what others thought. Finally the jail cell door began to open. I experienced the connection and the intimacy that was taking place with guests in my home as I started to put impressions to rest.

I began to get rid of the trappings that made the jail cell so attractive—like filling our home with excessive details, many of which went unnoticed and actually stole the joy of entertaining. I began adding special touches, and even added a theme to a party for the right event, but I always remember to keep my motives in check.

When it comes to décor, we need to look at our motivations: Are we adding special touches for ourselves, to prove to others that we're unique, special, outside-the-box, the best dinner-party queen around? We also have to remember how much all these time-consuming touches—often done in the wrong spirit and for the wrong reasons—take us away from our families.

The best way to impress others in your home is through genuine care and authenticity— something no killer centerpiece will ever do.

Once you've been outside the jail cell of perfectionism, the world looks so much better and you learn deep things about yourself and others. For example, you learn that your mistakes make you relatable. People can see themselves in you and sense that you have a lot in common. Honestly, do you relate to people who have no flaws? It's impossible to have a real conversation with such a person because we can't see ourselves in them.

Some time ago we hosted a friend's fiftieth birthday party. Everything was going great, and people were laughing and enjoying a really good meal. But as the party was about to end, I saw something that almost made my heart stop: melted red wax running down the wall. I'd forgotten to clean it up after our last dinner party. I know people saw it, because later that night a guest who was new to our

*People tend
to relax more
in imperfect
settings than
perfect ones.* home said to me, "I'm so glad you have wax on your wall.
It's so refreshing to be in a home that isn't perfect." What
she was really saying, but not in so many words, is that she
found our life relatable to hers, and as a result she was able
to relax and really enjoy herself, which is one of the many
gifts of real entertaining and hospitality.

NEVER APOLOGIZE

One of the most helpful pieces of advice I've received that helped me battle
perfectionism is to never apologize for a culinary mistake. This may sound
contrary to what it means to be a hospitable hostess, so let me explain. When
we apologize for part of a meal that is still good but not up to our standards
(some of which are still stained by perfectionism), we are actually stealing
the potential enjoyment that our guests would otherwise experience. The
fact is, most of the time guests are so focused on the moment, so grateful to
get away from the daily grind and to relax, that they don't notice culinary
shortcomings. So by apologizing, we are pointing out things that most people
wouldn't even notice. And if they do notice it, most really don't think it's a
big deal. Oftentimes, pointing out a defect in a meal is more about us and
not about our guests at all.

Years ago we invited two couples and their kids to come to our house
for dinner for the first time. I was going to wow them, really show them
what a great hostess I was even as I greeted them at the front door with
our two toddlers and six-month-old underfoot. I'm sure I even declined
their offer to bring part of the meal, because again, I was prideful in having to do it all.

During this particular meal I served chicken divan, a very simple,
crowd-pleasing dish you can prepare the night before and then pop in the
oven shortly before it's time to serve.

I should have put my pride away before I opened the front door that
night. I was nervous and excited at the same time. But I put too much into
my own human efforts, trying to make things too perfect. It added the
weight of the evening on my shoulders, as if it were all about me, instead
of allowing an authentic experience to unfold. I really needed to remove
myself and let the night flow without involving my pride.

When I served the meal that night, complete with rice and broccoli on the side, I was so proud of how beautiful the plate looked. Adding a twig of rosemary to the dish made it appear restaurant-worthy. I just knew the tender, mouth-watering chicken would melt in my guests' mouths.

After everyone was served, I sat down with a sigh of relief. Yes! I did it! But then I cut into my chicken and saw pink—pink meant raw! I forgot to precook the chicken! How did I miss this small detail when I'd cooked this recipe so many times before?

Once a perfectionist doesn't mean always a perfectionist. Give yourself room to change and grow—it usually comes with age.

I was mortified and apologized over and over. I quickly and even aggressively gathered all the plates back into the kitchen. My husband was clued in to what happened—the sharp look in my eye was hard to miss—and he helped me out. We nuked each plate and re-served the guests in a not-so-happy manner.

I was embarrassed and sick inside. What did I learn? To check your food before you serve it? Sure. But also to realize mistakes happen and to go with the flow. And that a microwave is a hostess's best friend.

But I learned something more. By profusely apologizing, I made a not-so-bad situation even worse. I sucked the joy from the room that evening. The lighthearted mood became overshadowed by a negative spirit just like that.

PERFECTIONISM FOSTERS LONELINESS AND ISOLATION

There is a deeper reason why it's imperative that we combat perfectionism in our lives. When we strive to make hospitality perfect instead of excellent, we isolate ourselves from others. Perfectionists have a hard time making and keeping friends. They are not very happy because they know they will never be able to live up to their own unrealistic expectations. And our unrealistic expectations can actually hurt those around us, because they feel they can never measure up.

My parents were good role models. Our home did not have to be perfect before they invited people in. And they always included my sisters and me by having us help get ready, cook, and set the table—mistakes and all. We witnessed the benefits and happiness that living a hospitable life brought to our parents. Their happiness did not revolve around perfection. It was a matter of the heart.

But my background is very different from that of many other women. On a flight home from the Midwest, I struck up a conversation with a lady on the plane and we started talking about reluctant entertaining. With tears in her eyes, she told me how she tried to entertain earlier in her marriage, but by the time company would arrive, she'd be sick. She'd run around the house all day, trying to make everything perfect, until she literally became ill. She said she had a perfectionist mother who held impossible standards, especially for a working mother. To her, entertaining was a jail cell—not the enjoyable garden that included the deep connection with other people that she wanted it to be.

So now her family has resorted to eating out. When it's their turn to entertain, they head to a restaurant. These bad feelings haunt her to this day. Her children will likely feel the same way, which is one of the main reasons I set out to write this book: to set families free from the generational jail cell of perfectionism and isolation.

Think about kids. They don't start out in life being perfectionists. They learn from us. To this day I still struggle with wanting the kitchen to be perfectly cleaned or the kids' beds to be made before their friends arrive. But I know the perfect family does not exist—at least not in my home. Our imperfections and the little messes that surround us make us much more relatable when others come to visit.

When Abby decided to bake a cake for her brother's friend David, she got right in the kitchen and started baking. I backed off from helping out because I wanted it to be her thing, not mine. Abby had one goal in mind: to practice what she had been taught—hospitality. Sure, the kitchen was an utter disaster when

Photo courtesy of Tim Tidball Photography

she finished, and as I looked over at the lopsided cake, I just had to smile.

She was determined to make her own frosting, adding homemade strawberry jam to it. And even though the cake was far from perfection, I'd have to say the taste was *perfecto*! As we gathered in the living room with a bunch of teenage boys, Abby brought out the cake lit with candles and we all sang. The homemade cake, imperfect as it was with icing dripping down the sides, was not the focus. The focus was making David feel special on his birthday.

It's hard to relate to people who give the impression that their life is perfect because regular individuals can't relate to perfect people.

Success is defined when our children and their friends can relate, laugh, engage, and see beyond themselves. Our place is often messy, but it doesn't matter because our kids are reaching out and sharing what they have in the best way they know how.

Things don't have to be perfect in order to share our lives with others. I'm still learning this lesson, and my hope is our kids are catching on too!

THE REAL DEFINITION OF FEAR

When it comes to hospitality, fear needs a new and more accurate definition. Years ago I gained an insight into the joy-stealing nature of fear, an insight that improved my ability to get to the soul of hospitality. This better definition, which we have taught to our children many times, is a helpful acronym: **F**alse **E**vidence **A**ppearing **R**eal.

We all have a fear of rejection in some way. Maybe we're worried about our food not turning out, worried about what to say to our guests, worried about initiating new friendships in general because they might not like us as much as we like them. We just spend a lot of time worrying and fretting over situations that are simply false but appear real. Our imagination goes wild before the event even takes place; we're held back by a fear of something that never becomes real.

One example would be, "What if they don't like us?" I've heard that over and over from hostesses, and I have felt this same fear as well. But more than likely your guests do like you and are honored to be invited into your home, and chances are they will prove it by inviting you into theirs.

And in the rare case that your guests do not reciprocate, well, that just happens sometimes. It's okay. Some people just don't connect with each other. We can't allow the fear of possible disappointment to rob us of the future happiness that entertaining can bring us.

OVERCOME IF/THEN THINKING

Another pitfall that stops us from hospitable entertaining is similar to perfectionism. As I mentioned in chapter 2, many women are hounded by the pitfalls of wishful-thinking joy busters. They have a dangerous if/then way of thinking: "I'll be happy when . . . my house is clean, I have that new house, I have a larger house, my yard is finished, that wall is painted, I have more money, my kids are older, my marriage is better, I have that new kitchen. . . ."

We tend to have the unhealthy view that things need to be just right before we can open up our lives to others. I struggled with this if/then thinking with my kitchen. *If* I could just remodel my kitchen, *then* I would entertain more.

For the first four years we lived in our current house, we had a small, outdated kitchen. Our family could barely maneuver around; it was a disaster if two or more were cooking in the same area. The appliances were dying and the cupboards and the floor were falling apart. I found it interesting how friends weren't afraid to say, "You need a new kitchen!"

But I didn't let it stop me from being hospitable. If I had given in to the if/then thinking, four years of family memories would never have been created. Rather than lock myself in the if/then prison, I dealt with the fear (which was not real) of what people would think of me. If I hadn't, it would have been a very unfruitful place for my family and me to remain.

Another way I learned to overcome this if/then thinking was to set more realistic, achievable goals. By inviting fewer people to dinner at a time, I was able to let go of my perfect and big thinking and let small and more intimate moments take over. Again, I learned to go with the flow, which helped me branch out of my comfort zone.

OVERCOME: LET GO OF RIGIDITY

Sometimes we also have to sacrifice our usual ways of doing something—possibly even the way we were raised to do it—to learn a new and better way. Rigidity can squelch our joy, make us sick, and ruin our friendships. It's actually one of the silent killers of hospitality, and for that matter, marriage. As a newlywed, I was stubborn in the ways I did certain things; I had to learn to compromise with my new husband in the ways he did things. I had a certain idea of how I wanted to entertain, and he had another. We were two lives coming together, trying to create a blended style. It was frustrating for me.

Eventually I realized that there is not always one certain way to do something and that life is constantly changing and shifting. It was a learning process that freed me up, and I became a different person. I also learned to relax more as a young mother; my patience level completely changed. I realized that I couldn't afford to be so unrealistic with my expectations anymore, especially with children on my hips. So I came up with these two questions that helped gauge my attitude: (1) Do I want to be miserable? (2) Do I want my family to learn to be miserable?

Keeping these two thoughts in the back of my mind helped me learn to bend and to make changes more easily. Like when my guests showed up late or even canceled at the last minute. Or when our kids would get sick or misbehave. Or when our guest's daughter had an accident in her sleep, soaking our couch. Or worse yet, when my mistake with a knife changed the whole course of the evening.

One night, as our guests arrived right on time, I was cutting the last-minute veggies for our salad. The knife sliced deep into my left hand, and blood began oozing everywhere. We made the quick decision that my friend Liz would accompany me to the emergency room, and the dads would stay behind, continue the meal, and get the five kids fed.

Be open to change before rigidity steps up and kills what you love.

When Liz and I returned hours later, our night was shot. The sit-down dinner never happened, and we found the dirty dishes already piled up on the counter. I learned a lesson in flexibility that night—forced to accept a situation that was completely different from what I had envisioned for this perfect intimate dinner party. But our friends understood, and that was important.

OVERCOME: THE POWER OF LAUGHTER

Laughter is a gift from God. It's an expression that comes deep from the heart and helps us to let go of perfection-born fears. I remember the cold winter's night when my husband was traveling and I decided to invite some friends and their daughters to dinner. When Kristi broke her tooth while biting into a crunchy piece of bread, I was initially embarrassed and felt bad for her misfortune. But we turned the situation into a laughable moment. We even got the camera and took a picture of how funny she looked. That night became a story to remember. In cases like that, releasing a stressful situation by laughing actually feels good and frees everyone from embarrassment.

Entertaining with laughable moments can impact and create history with our families and our friends. Even when mistakes happen, they can turn into fond "Remember when" memories.

One of those moments was back in 2005, when our family entertained sixty guests for a sit-down dinner party in our backyard. The celebration

was for my husband's new book, *No More Christian Nice Guy*. Just when everything was going smoothly, this disaster took our family off guard.

Some guests were filing through the buffet line, and many had already seated themselves in chairs around the tables. Then we all heard it, a loud *pssshhh* sound coming from . . . where?

Instantly my husband and I made eye contact.

The sprinklers!

As if he were in the fifty-yard dash, Paul darted across the yard faster than I'd ever seen him run on the soccer field and quickly shut off the sprinklers. We were fortunate that the water started over by the kids' table (Whew! Kids like action, right?) and hit only a few of our adult guests.

In the past I would have been mortified. But now this story goes down in Coughlin history as a "Remember when." Even our guests made light of the situation that night, as laughter became good medicine and the night was labeled a fond memory.

OVERCOME: WHEN GOOD IS ENOUGH

Only two weeks after moving into her new home, with many possessions still in boxes, my friend Carrie decided to host a dinner party to celebrate my new book contract. Carrie hosted twelve people for a memorable evening and celebration, one that I will never forget. I was touched not only by her kind gesture but by her courage to overcome what we envision to be good or perfect.

As Carrie went to set the table for this large group, she couldn't find her entertaining pieces, napkins, table settings, etc., that were still packed away. What Carrie did next was simple. Letting go of perfect ideas, she headed quickly to the nearest Goodwill to find what she needed to finish setting her table. The table had mismatched napkins and plates, and no one even noticed, myself included (until she pointed it out to me later).

This is another example of the true meaning of hospitality. In this case, it wasn't about the perfect meal or table setting, but about a night of supportive friends coming together to share in the joy and to encourage me with the task ahead. The feeling of togetherness, during the meal and after dinner, is most memorable in my mind. Our discussion turned into liveliness and substance, talking about heartfelt struggles in our families. Some of us knew each other better than others, but by the end of the evening I'd say the beauty of hospitality shone through. We could all call each other friend.

Carrie's dinner party could have very easily been squelched that night. She could have locked herself into the jail of perfectionism, calling the whole party off because things were not "good enough." But Carrie knew better. She quickly overcame by deviating and coming up with a new plan.

OVERCOME: GAIN COURAGE

Sometimes hospitality requires more courage than we feel we possess. Possibly you're one who could raise her hand and say, "Yes, I could use a dose of more courage!" My husband writes and speaks about what grows and shrinks courage in our everyday lives. Often, I shied away from courage because I knew that it would be disruptive to my life, that it would knock me out of my safety zone. I wanted comfort.

Sometimes we love safety so much that it stifles us. And then we don't grow beyond a certain point, which means we miss out on many of life's blessings. Hospitality is one of those life blessings.

So I learned more about courage as I matured and started emulating people I admired who had it. I realized some unhealthy patterns that weren't working for me, and I learned to be more courageous by pushing past my fears. One act of courage for me was to start my blog, Reluctant Entertainer, and to be real and authentic with readers by sharing my entertaining philosophy. I've also been inspired by my husband's book *Unleashing Courageous Faith*. Some key points of his helped me, and I've adapted and included them in the sidebar on the next page because I think they will benefit you when it comes to opening up and sharing your life with others.

Gaining more courage helps you to love more. It helps put fears, worries, and imperfections aside, and you're able to love more deeply. I've learned that courage doesn't just come to you. It takes effort and willingness, and it often puts you at risk.

COURAGEOUS HOSPITALITY

1. Know that you are valuable and important to God, and made in His image.
2. Know that you are unique and that people want to know you more.
3. Focus your will into something meaningful (relationships!).
4. Lean into your fears; learn that things do not have to be perfect.
5. Learn that people usually don't care about the things that bother you.
6. Learn to take a small hill. Start small and invite people into your life!
7. Make soul-friends, friends who get what you are all about.
8. Love the unlovely. Does it really matter what your house looks like?
9. Combat materialism. You don't need the newest or the best.
10. Combat cynicism, which can drain us of hope, creativity, and energy—all building blocks for courage.

OVERCOME: SURROUND YOURSELF WITH IMPERFECT PEOPLE

The best thing I ever did in fighting perfectionism was to surround myself with imperfect people. I found friends with messy houses, dirty toilets, unorganized closets and cupboards, and better yet, imperfect kids. I became healthier and more courageous to be myself when I realized that we're all real people living imperfect lives.

After a night out with special friends, the best part of the evening was going back to their beautiful, lived-in home. We took our shoes off and headed to the family room, where we lounged and put our feet up, allowing our bodies to sink deep into the cushions, and we just hung out, reveling in the time together. Even though this home was spectacular in size and décor, it was still homey. Most of us would agree that when you walk into a lived-in home, you feel more at ease, more at home.

So when it comes to our homes, our cooking, our entertaining style, I think of my blogging friend Nester and how she encourages the imperfect:

"Maybe we eat on paper plates, maybe we are out of napkins. No one seems to notice that part. Sometimes, showing some imperfections allows people to feel more at ease. I'm so glad that it doesn't have to be perfect to be beautiful or meaningful or delicious!"

Chicken Divan

My friends Jane and Carol Ann shared this recipe with me in my early entertaining days, and it became one of my "standby" dishes to cook for company. You can make it a day in advance and refrigerate it until you're ready to bake it. Serves 6 to 8.

6 boneless, skinless chicken breasts, precooked and cut in half (for 12 pieces)
2 cans cream of chicken soup, undiluted
1 cup mayonnaise
1 tsp. lemon juice
¼ cup white wine or sparkling apple cider
1 to 2 tsp. curry powder (to taste)
1 tsp. tarragon (to taste)
½ cup grated sharp cheddar cheese
1 cup bread crumbs
Cooked rice

Preheat oven to 350°F.

Spray a 9" x 13" pan with nonstick cooking spray. Arrange precooked chicken in the pan. Combine the soup, mayonnaise, lemon juice, wine, curry, and tarragon and pour over the chicken. Sprinkle the cheese and bread crumbs over the top. Bake for 40 minutes. Serve over cooked rice.

OVERCOME: EYES ON THE PERFECT ONE

So when we're relaxed and all eyes are off of perfect, when we take courage a step further by focusing on what really matters and then moving forward with it, we find ourselves catching a ray of hope. I know, because when I read about it or see it practiced firsthand, I find myself saying, "I want that!"

We long for a picture of hope, a perfect role model, something to look up to as we aim to get away from this unhealthy pattern of perfectionism ingrained in our thinking and stuck in our minds. Where do we turn for help to get us out of this jail cell of perfectionism? My answer is simple: We quit looking at others and turn our hope to the Perfect One, as Edith Schaeffer reminds us in *The Hidden Art of Homemaking*:

> *The only artist who is perfect in all forms of creativity—in technique, in originality, in knowledge of the past and future, in versatility, in having perfect content to express as well as perfect expression of content, in having perfect truth to express as well as perfect expression of truth, in communicating perfectly the wonders of all that exists as well as something about Himself, is of course God—the God who is Personal.*

However great or perfect we think we are, what we're trying to accomplish will never be perfect. And that is okay, because we were never created to be that way. So when we look around the dinner table with our friends, and we see a spot on the tablecloth, or crumbs on the floor because we didn't have time to vacuum before our guests arrived, or a burnt edge around the crust, we realize that freedom of the imperfect is what helps us to become that gracious hostess we long to be. It helps us to overcome, to open up, and to take risks. I'd say it's the foundation of hospitality, by looking to the Perfect One.

Easy Press Piecrust for Strawberry Pie

This piecrust recipe came from my friend Mary years ago. I've included the recipe for a strawberry pie, but the crust can also be used for banana cream pie (see p. 146.) or any in-season berries or peaches. Try serving your pie in individual ramekins—one for each guest.

Easy Press Crust:
½ cup oil
2 T. milk
1½ cups flour
¼ cup sugar
1 tsp. salt

Preheat oven to 375°F. Whip oil and milk together with a fork. Mix dry ingredients together and add to oil and milk. Mix with a fork until well blended. Press into pie pan and poke with a fork. Bake 12 to 15 minutes.

Variation: Press in the bottom of a 9" x 13" pan.

Strawberry Pie Filling:
1 cup sugar
1 cup water
2 T. cornstarch
3 T. dry strawberry gelatin
2 pints fresh strawberries
whipping cream, whipped
Easy Press Crust, prebaked

In medium saucepan, stir together sugar, water, and cornstarch. Cook on high, stirring constantly, until thick and clear. Stir in strawberry gelatin until it dissolves. Let glaze cool. Slice strawberries into piecrust. Pour cooled glaze over berries. Serve with whipped cream.

Simplifying Entertaining

Once you experience freedom from perfectionism, you'll find it's much easier to enjoy a simpler approach to entertaining, whether in a formal dinner party, a casual get-together, or even a small birthday party. You may even find yourself redefining what entertaining means to you.

For example, for many hosts, once the monkey of perfectionism is off their back, they realize that planning all the details for a gathering is stressful and sometimes unnecessary. They soon realize that simplifying isn't just easier but better because it allows them to focus on their guests more. Instead of trying to cook the entire meal, they may opt for takeout and serve it on their own dishes, and as a result have a more relaxed time with their guests. Now, that sounds inviting, doesn't it?

The secret to a successful get-together is simplicity, planning ahead, and being relaxed and engaged when you greet your guests at the front door—something that often does not happen when there are too many details to sweat about.

A simpler approach will help you enjoy your guests more, without a whole lot of fuss or formality and without feeling like you're a slave in your own kitchen. One night, my guests arrived early

four

and I was not prepared. I was flustered and irritated when they came into the kitchen to talk to me, and worse yet, when they offered to help, I said no. I didn't want them there—I wanted them out in the living room waiting for the perfect moment when I'd burst into the room with warm and glowing appetizers. Instead I was still picking up, preparing, and cleaning. I was not a happy hostess.

Honestly, I still struggle with keeping my parties simple—planning too much food, not sticking to my original guest list, not being familiar with my recipes, spending more than I can afford, or not having a timeline to keep me on track. So when guests arrive, I'm more frustrated than gracious. And sometimes when they arrive early, I even find myself thinking, *Why did I invite them in the first place?* Talk about being inhospitable.

Failing to honor the benefits of simplicity has unexpected consequences, and it's usually our guests who suffer from them. A couple years into our marriage, I started watching other hostesses whom I greatly admired. I watched their gracious, relaxed style. It was impressive how they came up with a simple yet tasty menu, how they weren't intimidated by guests contributing to the meal, and how their simple table setting was attractive without being elaborate. When hosted by one friend, Michelle, I looked around and saw a normal, lived-in home, but took note of a clean bathroom (one thing I've always tried to do before company comes). And more important, I saw how well she treated her husband. Her kids in general were very happy, and I watched how they connected with their guests. It was beautiful and freeing to know that I could try to be that way. So I took what I learned and implemented it into my own style of entertaining.

Here are some simpler keys to entertaining that I've learned the hard way, and it's my pleasure to share them with you.

SIMPLE INVITE

The first aspect of planning a dinner party is deciding who will come to dinner. The fact is we usually can't have everyone we want over at the same time. Someone is not going to be invited.

First, consider whom your family wants to have, and don't agonize over the list. Start with people you haven't seen in a while, friendships you'd like to rekindle, maybe just two or three people. Keep your guests' personalities in mind and what interests they may share with you or other people you are inviting. Try running the guest list by your family members or a close friend if you're really in a bind and can't make a decision.

Don't budge from your original plan until you become a more seasoned hostess. Then you can let hospitality flow and be creative in last-minute changes.

If you have a hard time with conversation, invite someone who doesn't—someone who can help keep the conversation flowing without dominating it. You may even want to ask them in advance if they'd be willing to help you out. Many people like to offer a prayer before their meal, but some hostesses feel uncomfortable doing this, so choose someone who is at ease praying out loud as well.

If you have children, inviting their friends' parents is always a plus. Your kids will have fun, and you'll get a chance to find out what kind of influence the parents have on them. At the same time, think of people you know who are lonely and hurting. They will usually be quiet during your gatherings, so consider asking one of your more caring guests to strike up a conversation with this person. We have never had a guest say no to such an important assignment. Mix it up. Maybe invite an older couple and a younger couple. Remember singles too, as they are often left out of many social functions. You get great conversation going when you have a diverse mix of friends.

If you're married, you and your spouse should be making these invitation decisions together. It makes for a much more harmonious evening. I've received email after email from readers who found out the hard way that certain couples are not a good fit—maybe the two husbands didn't get along or had nothing in common. That can turn into an uncomfortable situation.

My husband and I have kept a running list of guests we'd like to have over. Some time ago we wrote down the names of people we wanted to pursue friendships with, with the goal of having them over for dinner. We dreamed for a bit about fostering these relationships.

You can invite a small group (easy) or a large group (takes a bit more work), but I prefer a mid-sized party of five or six people. My family and I don't live in a mansion, so I do feel I have to put limits on the size (unless we're entertaining outdoors, where we have more space).

Do you like the idea of tradition, inviting the same people to the same event every year? Or would you prefer to change it up? There may be circumstances where you feel obligated to invite, and that takes a gracious hostess with a good attitude, when in reality it might not be your first choice.

Once you've decided whom to invite (keeping a few alternates in case someone can't come), it's time to set a date that works best for you. Let your guests know as soon as possible.

SIMPLE MENU

Planning the menu is where many hostesses get hung up. Whether it's a lack of confidence in your cooking abilities or a matter of not having the time to research what menu to serve, there are some simple ways to overcome this roadblock.

Having two or three signature dishes—recipes you've prepared over and over—will free you of the stress of trying something new. Not knowing your recipe often results in spending more time in the kitchen than you had planned. That can be disastrous if you're on a tight schedule. My blogging friend Tsh offers this helpful advice: "Cook something you've already tried. I love experimenting with new recipes, but it's better to test them on your own kids and husband, not someone else's. Don't stress yourself out with

Zucchini Noodles With Parmesan Sauce

Don't know what to do with all those zucchini in the garden? This is the tastiest recipe, and even your kids will eat it. I can't count the number of kids who have learned to eat zucchini at our house! Serves 6 to 8.

Zucchini Noodles:
- 12 small zucchini
- 2 T. olive oil
- salt and pepper

Parmesan Sauce:
- 10 garlic cloves, pressed
- 2 T. olive oil
- 2 cups whipping cream
- 1 cup fresh, grated
  Parmesan cheese
- salt and pepper

With a potato peeler, create long, wide zucchini ribbons by starting at the top of each zucchini and peeling down the length of it. Turn after each peel to get all the green part first. Continue peeling until the center portion becomes too thin, and discard the rest.

Heat a large skillet on medium-high and add the olive oil and zucchini noodles. Sauté for approximately 2 to 3 minutes. Do not overcook or they will become soggy. Add salt and pepper to taste.

In a saucepan, sauté the pressed garlic in olive oil. Add the whipping cream, turn the heat to high, and stir until it begins to boil. Then turn the heat down to low and simmer for 10 minutes. Remove from the heat and stir in the Parmesan cheese, salt, and pepper. Pour over the "noodles" and serve.

Variation: Substitute any kind of pasta for the zucchini noodles.

Figure out your top three signature meals. Tape the recipes and details inside your kitchen cupboard or in a place that you can easily access. Eventually you'll have them memorized.

the unknown of your culinary results—go with a menu you've tried at least twice."

My favorite entertaining menu is salmon, zucchini noodles, salad, and bread. And of course a fabulous dessert to top it off. I serve salmon year-round, grilling it in the summer and broiling it in the winter. My friend Barb serves home-raised, grass-fed lamb. Another friend, Vicky, specializes in Thai food, while my sister Diane can master any meat and potato recipe. My sister Linda makes our family recipes—*Fleisch-kuechle* (a German meat and dough recipe) just like our mom and Grandma Dubs made, and zwieback (dinner rolls) like Grandma Friesen made. My dad makes annual New Year's cookies (a deep-fried donut rolled in sugar), and close to fifty friends help to celebrate New Year's Day around these tasty treats. Everyone just seems to have a food specialty.

I feared serving the same dish twice to my guests, so I came up with a simple system using three-by-five index cards. I write my guest's name at the top of a card and record the date of the event and what

I served. At a quick glance I can see what I've already served to whom. It also gives me ideas for new guests—reminders of full menus I've served successfully before, what dishes went well together, etc.

It's the responsibility of my guests to tell me ahead of time if they have an allergy. And my card system is a great way to keep track of them. When it comes to pickiness, I figure people can pick out what they don't like, but if I have a note on the card—for example, I know that our friend Bill doesn't like cherries—then it's a good reminder.

The Internet is a great resource for finding quick, easy, simple meals. If you're savvy with a computer, and even if you're not, it's easy to orga-

Kraft's iFood Assistant is an iPhone application that helps in food planning and meal preparation, including creating a shopping list when you're on the go.

The Leftover Wizard at BigOven.com suggests recipes based on any three ingredients you choose. This site is creative fun!

SuperCook.com is a recipe search engine that utilizes the ingredients you already have on hand. It creates your recipe right before your very eyes as you enter ingredients.

RecipeMatcher.com is a site where you type in the ingredients you've got, and it gives you a long list of recipes that include at least one of those ingredients.

The Ingredients tab at AllRecipes.com allows you to include ingredients that you want in one list and exclude in the other.

nize files right on your desktop to save your favorites for easy access. Sites like AllRecipes.com, Cooks.com, BettyCrocker.com, Kraft.com, and ThePioneerWoman.com are some of my favorites.

I'm using the Internet more and more, which means I'm using my cookbooks less and less. But I still love them and have my favorites. I like to use three-ring binders and sheet protectors for storing and organizing my recipes.

Your simple goal is to put good food on the table and to have a good time. Evaluate what's in your freezer and what you want to purchase—don't overspend on your budget. Don't forget the simplicity of buying ready-made food, or even a roasted chicken from the local grocery store. Serve it with a salad and a fresh loaf of bread.

When appropriate, delegate portions of the meal. It will help with your budget and your time. I try to have the menu organized before I make the invite, so when guests ask what to bring I'm ready to give an answer. If I don't know what I'm serving, I'll delegate bread and drinks. If you know your guest is a non-cook, definitely give them something easy to contribute. Decide if you want your guests to bring their food already on a platter, ready to serve, or if they can assemble it or heat it in your kitchen.

SIMPLE PLAN

With your guest list, date, and menu nailed down, it's time to plan and organize. Not having a plan can make a hostess miserable, creating a domino effect on the family. I prefer an easy organized system of notebooks and making lists for ideas, goals, menus, and shopping lists. I even use a notebook to jot down the things I don't want to forget and record the chores I want to complete.

Seeing a prepared table or serving area gives your guests a relaxed feeling the minute they walk into your home.

Create a timeline by working backward from the party date. Decide when the shopping will be done, which chores can be completed ahead of time and who is responsible for them, what food can be prepared in advance, and so on. Whether your party is days or weeks away, having a firm timeline in place will help prevent last-minute panic.

If you have children, get them involved. Give everyone a chore or two. In our home, entertaining is usually a family affair, so I'll often write down what I want my kids to help out with. It's great to include the family, because then the night becomes their night too, not just mine as the hostess.

SIMPLE SETTING

Begin to think about your space—your table, the number of available chairs, whether the outdoors is an option—and how it will best accommodate your party, the meal you plan to serve, and the mood you want to set. Do you want to serve the meal at the table or have guests sit around the living room to eat?

If you plan to set the food up buffet style, get your plan in place, and if you'll need extra tables, get them out early. Every Fourth of July we invite a large group over and use our dining room table as the buffet. A wider table is useful, allowing plenty of room to display the food but also leaving some space around the edge where guests can set their plates down and free up their hands. Choose an area for your guests to start, with napkins, silverware, and plates, and position the food in the order it will be used—for example, if you have hamburgers or hot dogs, place the buns before the meat and the condiments after.

Setting a pretty table can be simple. Don't worry about overcomplicating the table by trying to make it too formal. Start with choosing a tablecloth (or placemats) and napkins, then add in the plates, flatware, and glasses. I put the bread or salad plate to the left. Forks go on the left of the dinner plate and your knife and spoon on the right. If you're serving soup or salad, the salad fork goes on the outside left and the soup spoon on the outside right. The water goblet goes above the knife, and if you're serving wine, the wine glass goes to the right of that.

Finish off the table with a simple, low-profile centerpiece, like garden flowers and candles. Anything tall or too large can be a distraction. Over-the-top fancy takes away from what simple should be.

PARTY TIME

The day of a dinner party can be very exciting, or it can be very daunting and stressful. I hate to admit it, but sometimes I've yelled at my family the day of the event because of my lack of organization. So early on I learned a little secret to help me stay on track. I mentioned above the importance of creating a timeline for the days or weeks leading up to the event. Well, I do the same thing for the day of the event, working backward from the time guests are set to arrive. This helps me prioritize what needs to be done and in what order, giving me goals to work toward to avoid any time crunch. Ideally, I try to allow one hour to relax before guests arrive. Believe it or not, it *can* happen if you plan for it!

I like to make my first task of the day setting the table. Glancing over to see a set table gives a boost of confidence as I prepare throughout the day. Clean or tidy up bathrooms early in the day; don't save it for last. Thinking ahead about what to wear is important too, so you don't find yourself rummaging through your closet at the last minute.

Last-minute runs to the grocery store can be maddening for any hostess. This is why grocery lists are a must early in the process. If possible, substitute an ingredient with another in order to avoid running to the store.

Savory Oregon Salmon

This marinade is delicious and can be prepared under the broiler or on the barbecue grill. Serves 8.

1 or 2 skinless salmon fillets (2 lbs.) or 8 salmon steaks
¼ cup olive oil
¼ cup vegetable oil
½ cup soy sauce
1 clove garlic,
½ tsp. ground ginger
juice of 1 lemon
3 T. seafood seasoning

Combine marinade ingredients and blend well. Pour the marinade into a zipper bag. If necessary, cut the fish into pieces that will fit in the marinade bag. Add the fish to the marinade, squeeze the air out of the bag, and seal it. Refrigerate for 4 to 8 hours, turning occasionally. (If you marinate overnight, a very strong flavor results.)

To broil: Heat broiler to high. Place salmon on a broiler pan and cook 6 minutes on each side, until the salmon is firm. Press the back of a spatula onto the salmon to feel for firmness. Once firm, the salmon is cooked. If it feels spongy, it is not fully cooked.

To grill: Prepare low coals in a charcoal grill, or set a gas grill to low heat. Layer two 18-inch pieces of foil (one directly on top of the other) and fold up each side about an inch to create a rectangular "tray." Place the tray on the grill over indirect heat. Lay the salmon fillet(s) on top of the foil and pour the marinade onto the fish. Cover the grill and cook 20 to 30 minutes. Do not turn the fish when grilling like you would when broiling. Check for doneness using a spatula, as described above.

And when a store run is unavoidable, consider sending someone other than you.

It's not the worst thing to be working in the kitchen when your guests arrive. After greeting them at the door, you can always invite them into your kitchen to join you, even giving them a light task to help out.

Last summer we invited two families over for a very simple dinner outside. They were families we don't socialize with often because of busy schedules, so we were really enjoying reconnecting with one another— adults and kids.

After dinner and dessert, we moved from the back patio to inside the house. Our son was playing the piano, and we mingled more and listened to the music. The night went longer than I had planned, but as we continued to lounge and go deeper in conversation, I knew this relaxed moment was not about me. It was significant. The moment was about the way our guests were engaging and how memories were being made with our teenage kids as they interacted.

Looking back, this was a successful, simple night! I had a plan, I kept the menu simple (I served a recipe I had cooked over and over), the guests

brought dishes, and my family jumped in and helped. I really enjoyed myself that evening because my intention was to keep it simple. In a way it was freeing to me, as I let go of the complicated and became a more effective hostess. My home felt warmer, and I'd go as far as saying it even had a glow to it. I'd love for you to consider this same effect happening in your own home as you invite others in. By watching your attitude change, you'll be amazed at what it does to your family. Often the result is more than we will ever comprehend, sometimes with eternal significance, possibly with an impact we'll never understand. Hospitality, in a mysterious way, does reduce down to love, doesn't it?

Discovering Your Inner Martha

There are so many different styles and ideas on entertaining that they can make your head swirl if you let them. A woman's entertaining style is shaped by the culture she lives in, how she was raised, her husband's or friends' influence, and more. I know that my entertaining style has changed over the years. Like many young women, I started off married life as a fairly modest entertainer. Then I swung to a more formal approach, trying to get fancy and impressive, not realizing that the exhaustion of it all was killing me. It was too much work (coming up with party favors or other over-the-top special details) and not enough reward because I was so busy in the kitchen or trying to keep the next course on track. I was not enjoying my guests like I should. Once I figured this out, I went back to a very simple yet elegant style of entertaining. It almost feels like you've arrived home when you discover your style and you're comfortable with it.

Hospitality should be a part of our spiritual DNA, because once you start practicing and living a hospitable life, it goes deeper into your soul. It seems when you're not living it, life feels very selfish in a way. It's easy to get into a rut of not allowing yourself to be creative or to look for new, fresh ways of giving. Beth Moore, in her

book *Get Out of That Pit*, was inspiring to me when I read her challenge to rethink creativity:

Once you become secure with who God made you to be, reaching out to others becomes much easier.

Created in the image of God, we are meant to brim over with creativity. Yes, that means you. Don't tell me you're not the creative type. I'm not talking right-brained-versus-left-brain drivel. I'm not talking accountant types versus actor types. All image-bearers of God were intended to overflow with effervescent life, stirring and spilling with God-given vision.

Our imaginations were fashioned like wicks to be ignited by the fire of fresh revelation, dripping with wax that God can imprint with His endless signatures. He writes in fonts and shades we've yet to see, telling us who He is, and what He's capable of doing. We were meant to see ourselves as part of something so much bigger than we are. Something vital. Something incredibly thrilling.

WHAT INSPIRES YOU?

Let's say you don't have a clue about what your style is, and you don't even know where to start. What inspires you? What makes you tick, gets you excited, makes you dream?

One thing I like to tell young hostesses is that it's okay to copy someone you admire or who inspires you. Maybe you're waiting in the doctor's office and thumbing through a magazine when an appealing look catches your eye. Make note of it, write it down in a notebook (or ask if you can rip out the page), and then replicate that idea.

This is why I like do-it-yourself projects—the idea often originates somewhere else, but you make the project into your own by using what you have. A simple centerpiece on the table can be exactly that. Foliage and even some pretty weeds are popular for decorating. Arrange your finds in a vase or lay them right

MAYBE SOME OF THESE IDEAS WILL INSPIRE YOU:

Comfort dinner: Any gathering of friends or family together over a meal, "just because," is satisfying and feels right, especially when simple comfort foods like lasagna, spaghetti, or roasted chicken are served.

Summer barbecue: This is my favorite way to entertain, because we can take advantage of homegrown foods and flowers from our garden or the local farmers' market to create a simple meal on the grill, and nature comes to light.

Appetizer or dessert: This is a classy way to entertain a large group of people without the formality of a sit-down dinner. Or make it a D.A.D. party—drinks, appetizers, desserts. It's even easier when everyone contributes.

Coffee or hot chocolate bar: This works later in the evening, where you provide desserts and your guests make their own drinks. It's cozy, warm, and informal.

Relaxing brunch: Everyone seems to pitch in and help put the food on the table when brunch is served. It doesn't have to be Sunday, of course, but it's usually a relaxing day with a light schedule. I prefer to prepare dishes ahead of time instead of on the day of the brunch.

Girlfriend party: This can be a casual buffet of sweet and savory foods or a potluck salad buffet, or a modern tea party with iced or hot teas and finger foods.

Takeout party: With so many gourmet food shops and restaurants around, takeout is perfect for a last-minute gathering—or even planned ahead if you know you'll be in a time crunch.

Open house. For any season or any occasion, an open house is a more informal—yet still elegant—way to host a larger group of people.

Outdoor party: Ambience seems to take care of itself when you're outside. Host a youth group, sports team, or birthday party.

Book club, game night, or fondue party: Conversation just happens at these informal, low-cost gatherings.

Change-it-up party: At my traditional New Year's Eve party, we change the seating of the guests with every course. It's a great way to ensure variety in conversation.

on your table amid a few tea light candles. Usually by taking your inspiration and moving forward with it, you'll have confidence and clarity.

To figure out your style of entertaining, consider various approaches and which ones appeal to you more. Do you prefer formal or informal, indoor or outdoor, buffet or sit-down dinners? Do you want to prepare it all yourself or make it potluck? Do you like tablecloths or placemats, and can you bend a bit when it comes to etiquette? Do you get stressed out with large groups and feel more comfortable with a more intimate gathering?

Probably the most important tip or advice I have to offer about finding the entertaining style that works for you is to not get wrapped up in comparing yourself to others. We're not all Martha Stewarts. Don't get bogged down with trying to impress and miss out on the whole purpose of entertaining in the first place: relationships. Don't try to be a hostess that you are not. You want to be gracious, and entertaining should feel natural.

COOKING INSPIRATION

Once you've come up with a style of entertaining that works for you—and you may need to experiment with a few different types—it's time to think about the food.

I was definitely influenced by my mother's cooking and the comfort recipes from her church cookbook years ago. Then Alton Brown came along, and his teachable cooking show was great entertainment for our entire family. Suzanne Somers was my hero in my thirties because, through her books, I learned to whip up sauces and some easy gourmet meals. And of course I appreciate Rachael Ray and her simple love for food. But eventually I found the best tried-and-true cookbook around, *The Best Recipe*, by the editors of *Cook's Illustrated* magazine. I learned to appreciate the accuracy and detailed information that helped me to become a better cook.

An easy way to get inspired comes by accepting a dinner invitation to someone's home, then admiring the hostess and her recipes, and eventually borrowing them. This is a form of compliment, something I've done many times. (Thank you, Di, Linda, Terri, Ginny, Faye, Jeannie, Michelle B., Cindy, Jenny, Kristi, Anne, and Pam.) Feel free to borrow ideas from friends who put a different spin on hospitality, who may take it further outside of a dinner party.

MAKE YOUR HOUSE A HOME

When it comes to entertaining, many women get hung up on the style of their home. If you don't have a particular style—and in fact, many women on my blog confessed they haven't found theirs yet—don't let it stop you from making your home a friendly place where people want to come and relax.

We strive to make our house open and inviting, even though it's not overly large. I've learned to work around the space issue to make people feel cozy. Comfort is what people are looking for, not the most elaborate or perfectly decorated.

So yes! Move on and get the house ready for company! Easy tips like these give you a few ideas to glance over, if you have the time, to make sure that your home is what you want it to be when your guests arrive.

- Experience the power of rearranging. It always makes a room feel brand-new. Invite a friend over with an entertaining eye to give you some tips.

- Scan a room, tidy up, and give the room a fresh touch of flowers or a basket of fresh fruit.

- Straighten your magazines. Reduce any clutter. Clean off your fridge.

- Use angles in decorating, arranging your furniture into conversation areas. Inside and outside!

- Use your family artwork around the house—it adds a warm feel.

- Use lamps in dark corners.

- Make sure your front porch is cleaned off with a seasonal feel to it.

- Tidy up the entryway, the first place your guests will see when they enter your house.

My blogging friend Melissa loves to decorate and create ambience in her home, but she's not crazy about cooking. In fact, she's told me she'd rather have a personal chef cooking all of her meals (I sometimes agree!), but she doesn't let it stop her from having guests over. She loves the process of creating a pleasant atmosphere—just like some women enjoy spending time preparing a new recipe.

My point is that some women completely enjoy decorating over cooking, or vice versa. It's rare to find women who can really do it all—and do it all well. So again, my advice is to keep it easy and light and make your home warm, cozy, and inviting. We know

If you're blessed with big and beautiful, learn to share it with others.

that hospitality is not about being the perfect family or entertainer. It can be as simple as offering a glass of water to a stranger or sitting on the front porch with your best friend.

ENTERTAINING ESSENTIALS

The items I have found to be the most useful for entertaining are ones I have collected over the years. They are foundational supplies for simple dinners or parties. On the next page I've included a list of basics, but remember my hospitality commandment #8, "Work with what you have." Build your stock of entertaining supplies as you're able. Get the colors or patterns of what you currently have down in your head, so when you're out shopping you can pick up bargain pieces or linens to tie in with your theme or style.

If you're just starting out, or happen to be in the market for new dishes, I recommend all white dishes and all clear glassware. They are practical for any season and any occasion, they allow for a wide range of options, and they eliminate indecisiveness, freeing you to spend your energy in other ways. And it's easier to find miscellaneous pieces at thrift stores, bargain stores, or yard sales. Think in terms of simple serving pieces adapted for a wide variety of uses, then add in accent side dishes of different colors. This is a nice way to use heirloom pieces too.

My Reluctant Entertainer blog icon is a discount store water goblet.

Not only did I pay just a dollar each for my set of twenty-six, but they are the perfect size for water, and they're classy and sturdy—I've yet to break one. I chose this dollar goblet as my blog icon because of the deeper meaning—that it's okay to buy at a discount store and it's smart to spend less money, and you can still set a beautiful table and share it with beautiful friends. Sometimes we just need to give ourselves permission to look for a bargain.

BASIC ENTERTAINING ITEMS

twelve place settings (dinner plates, salad/dessert plates,
appetizer plates, and bowls)

twelve water goblets

twelve coffee mugs

twelve flatware settings

one set of nesting mixing bowls

two large serving platters

two serving bowls

six votive candle holders

two to three small vases

one tablecloth

twelve cloth napkins

serving utensils (two large spoons, a carving knife and fork,
and salad servers)

one water pitcher

baking dishes (an oval and a 9" x 13")

barbecue tools and accessories

optional: appetizer forks, ice bucket and tongs, cake stands,
compote dishes, coffee or tea pots, napkin rings, ramekins

A few years ago I realized how charming it was to cook with ramekins. I was inspired to buy my first set of eight ramekins by friends in Wisconsin who are known for their hospitality, as they are constantly reaching out to people in the workplace, through ministries, and in their own community. We made a trip out to visit them, and when we sat down to a dinner for fourteen, I was so impressed with how they served the individual portions of lasagna—in a small aluminum loaf pan for each person. This was a fabulous and quick idea, and brilliant for cleanup, which has inspired me to keep individual servings in mind for lasagna, potpies, sweet potatoes, chocolate lava cake, and even fruit pies and cobblers. Miniature pans make guests feel as though you prepared the dish just for them!

Are you a placemat or tablecloth girl? According to a poll I conducted on my blog, twice as many people prefer tablecloths over placemats. My love for tablecloths started with my mother. When company came, we saw immediately how a table could be transformed. Tablecloths can be found

at discount stores, thrift stores, and yard sales, but my favorite ones were either gifts or were passed down, like my mom's beautiful white linen tablecloth that I will always cherish.

When buying a tablecloth, choose a color that will harmonize with the tableware you already own; if you frequently set up an extra table, you might look for two of the same tablecloth. Once I began hosting larger groups of people, I started buying two tablecloths in order to get a more uniform look.

This is an area where you can get creative too. I've used a shower curtain (bought at a yard sale, still in the package) or even bed sheets for covering a table. Most tablecloths have dual sides that are workable. One night when we had guests coming for dinner, I discovered my tablecloth had spots on one side, so I quickly flipped it over to the other side!

Storage for tablecloths and cloth napkins is easy: Keep them folded in a drawer or in a storage bin under your bed. Or do what I do and hang them in a coat closet. The secret is to have them pressed and ready for impromptu get-togethers. I also converted a wine cabinet into a napkin hutch, where I stash my favorite white cloth hotel napkins—which are classy, complement any table theme, and are easy to bleach. I also store paper napkins in this hutch because even with an elegant table setting, paper can work just fine.

Give yourself a couple of months to find what you are looking for at a yard sale before you buy brand-new. You'll be pleasantly surprised.

My advice to young entertainers is this: Get department and home decorator stores out of your head! It's not even necessary to spend money. A fun way to introduce variety is to swap and share entertaining pieces with a friend, especially if she has a certain set of dishes or a piece that fits your occasion. For my husband's thirty-fifth birthday, I hosted a sit-down dinner in my backyard.

My friend Anne and I pooled our white dishes together, and I borrowed her white table linen and some of her water goblets to mix in with my own. When my niece Addie holds showers for her friends, I let her go through my entertaining supplies and she borrows what she needs—like my cake stand and lid (which transforms into a punch bowl), or my large beverage jars and white platters.

When you think about how often certain entertaining pieces are used, isn't it better to borrow and share—and save money—than to have all the stuff in storage most of the time? This brings me to my philosophy on storage: Keep only key entertaining pieces on hand. Storing pieces that you use only once or twice a year takes up valuable space. If you find you really don't use something anymore, give it away.

YARD SALE TIPS FOR ENTERTAINING FINDS

My husband and I started our yard sale habit early on in marriage, after being influenced by Amy Dacyczyn's book *The Tightwad Gazette*. It became a healthy obsession for us, buying at one tenth the cost of retail prices and saving our family loads of money. Bargains make us feel accomplished and smart, like we're managing our money well.

The bulk of my entertaining supplies have been purchased at yard sales. A unique way to look at our savings is that we could afford to host dinner guests for an extra meal or two. It was a wise investment. Savings = Food = Friendship. Our savings became a gift to others.

Early on I put together a list of tips to help avoid buying too much junk or spending an endless amount of time looking for the "right bargain."

- Make a list of sales from your newspaper, craigslist, or another online source. Find neighborhoods you are comfortable with.

- Decide what you are looking for and what your budget is. Keep a list of needs in your purse and try not to stray from it.

- Put four to eight addresses on your list. Keep it simple!

- Go with a like-minded friend, one who'll give you constructive criticism regarding whether you need the item or whether it's a good buy!

- Limit yourself to one or two hours. There are more important things to do than shop yard sales all day.

- Every sale has a "sale-appeal" (like curb appeal). Learn to drive by and evaluate if it looks like one you want to shop.

- Marked prices: Learn to bargain. Ask for a lower price. It's okay to be assertive and make an offer.

- Non-marked prices: Decide what the item is worth to you, and then make an offer. It's risky to ask how much an item is, because the price may be much more than the item is worth.

- Be willing to walk away and to say no.

  - Be content with one find, especially if it's a good one.

When you're looking for entertaining items, keep your desired style and theme of how you like to entertain in mind. For instance, if you serve only buffet-style, look for pieces that would work for a buffet line. My eyes are always peeled for tablecloths or runners, unique candleholders, vases, decorating items, and folding chairs and tables.

Last summer my husband and I eyed this very cool round antique cooler. We agreed that it could be used for ice and drinks or as a plant stand. There was no price, so I offered five dollars and it was a done deal. In this case we were able to discuss if we needed this item, whether it was worth the money, and what we'd do with it. The benefit of having a friend with you is they can talk sense into you to not spend the money if it's something you really don't need.

DIY WITH CANNING JARS

My love for canning jars stretches back to the days when Grandma Dubs was alive. I remember how she'd cut fresh flowers from her garden and place them in a canning jar. You just can't make it simpler or more beautiful than that. But Grandma's real purpose for the jars was canning, which I rediscovered about ten years ago. I went on a hunt for jars at yard sales and came back with five boxes of quart-size jars, all for a dollar per box.

In this economy I find myself looking for new ways to reach out and bless others by rediscovering what I have, so the versatility of a canning jar works. Here are some of my favorite non-canning ways to use canning jars:

- Gifts like layer mixes (soups, cookies, and breads—see pp. 138–139) or a cake in a jar (p. 149)

- Drinking glasses—provide colored permanent markers for guests to write their names on their glasses

- Layer desserts like ice-cream sundaes, fruit parfaits, or layered Jell-O (kids love it!)

- A silverware holder when entertaining potluck- or buffet-style

- Candle holders or party lanterns (with tea lights or votives) to illuminate a walkway

- A vase to display fresh flowers, with water and small rocks at the bottom

- An herb vase—think in terms of scent by filling a jar with fresh rosemary or your favorite herb

STEP OUTSIDE YOUR "NORMAL" STYLE

Once you've learned more about your style and finding ways to let your creativity flow, I hope you can challenge yourself to give entertaining a try.

I think back to a hot summer's night when friends were coming over for dinner, and I warned them ahead of time to be prepared for a carefree evening. What was a carefree evening? I didn't plan to have the table set

Greek Salad on a Stick

This is an easy appetizer for any season! They can be kept at room temperature for up to an hour before serving. Serves 4 to 6.

> bamboo skewers
> ¼ pound feta cheese, cut into 16 small cubes
> 16 Kalamata olives, pitted
> 16 grape or cherry tomatoes
> 1 red onion, cut into 1-inch pieces
> 2 T. extra-virgin olive oil
> balsamic vinegar, to taste
> black pepper

Alternating between the feta, olives, tomatoes, and onions, thread 3 or 4 pieces of each onto a bamboo skewer. Layer the skewers on a platter and drizzle with olive oil and balsamic vinegar. Sprinkle with black pepper and serve.

Variation: Drizzle with Italian dressing.

Strawberry Pavlova and Cream

Serves 8.

6 egg whites
¼ tsp. cream of tartar
1 cup sugar
1 tsp. distilled white vinegar
1 tsp. almond extract
¼ cup cocoa
1 tsp. cornstarch
2 cups heavy whipping cream
¼ cup powdered sugar
2 T. Grand Marnier liqueur or 1 tsp. orange extract
2 pints strawberries, sliced

Preheat oven to 250°F. Line a baking sheet with parchment paper. Draw a 10-inch circle on the parchment.

In a large bowl, combine egg whites and cream of tartar. Beat at medium-high speed until foamy. Gradually beat in the sugar, a tablespoon at a time. Continue beating until stiff peaks form. Fold in the vinegar and almond extract.

In a small bowl, combine cocoa and cornstarch. Mix well and gently fold into the egg white mixture. Spoon this mixture onto the circle drawn on parchment paper. Bake for 1½ hours. Turn oven off and let meringue cool completely in the oven.

Beat the cream and powdered sugar until stiff peaks form. Add the liqueur or orange extract, mix, cover, and chill.

Just before serving, spoon the cream over the center of the meringue. Top with berries and serve.

or even the meal prepared, as I normally would have. I just wanted to relax with a game of Scrabble, and then later work in the kitchen with my friend Pam without a schedule or a ticking clock. When we did eventually get to the kitchen, we worked together chopping up fresh produce, slicing Pam's dill bread, and setting the salmon to marinate. What was really important was getting back to our game of Scrabble out on the back patio. As the guys took care of the grill, I snipped some flowers from the yard and quickly turned the tablecloth over to give a fresh feel. We brought out the dishes and set the table together, and it all seemed so effortless.

Planned dinners are very enjoyable and rewarding, especially when hard work is put into them. But this night I had a different style in mind. Stepping outside of my norm, I looked forward to this carefree evening all week because the payoff of everyone pitching in together was momentous. Perfection went out the door, and the clock was ignored.

My style of entertaining this night was exactly what I needed. I was reminded again how entertaining should be enjoyable. It shouldn't be stressful or overdone with a lot of fuss or formality, and you shouldn't feel exhausted. The end result should be like a magnet, where you sit down to the table and the food draws you to your guests.

Edith Schaeffer's style and honest approach to hospitality and relationships is still instructional for today's woman. It sparks the inspiration to pick and choose what works best for us. The bottom line is that we use our talents for the glory of God. In *The Hidden Art of Homemaking*, Schaeffer says,

> *Be satisfied with the fact that although your art or talent may never be accepted by the world as anything "great," and may never be your career, it can be used to enrich your day by day life: enrich it for you, and for the people with whom you live. And secondly, come to a recognition of the fact that it is important for you to be creative in this area to the extent of your talent: important for you as a person who is a creative creature.*

Engaging the Five Senses

My mother practiced a particularly effective strategy of hospitality, and if you were to ask her what it was, she probably couldn't tell you. Like so many women of her generation, she just knew it. She engaged all five of the senses when entertaining friends, acquaintances, and complete strangers, and I am so fortunate to have been there at the hem of her apron and soaking it all in.

Mom never entertained perfectly, and as you know by now, she didn't try. Instead, she entertained beautifully, meaning she loved the people more than the place settings. She wasn't showy, but she knew how to create a table where people felt loved.

Our home always smelled so delicious when guests came to the door and were greeted by my dad. He loved choosing a style of music to enjoy, usually gospel or classical. Both my parents knew how to carry a conversation and enter into the lives of others in our home, making their guests want to return time and time again. Mom taught my sisters and me how to set the table, which didn't require perfection, and when you walked through her front door you just felt hospitality.

My father married Ginny after my mother died, and fortunately for me, Ginny is also an accomplished hostess who believes

in genuine hospitality. I have been so fortunate to have two women from whom I have learned so much, and I have the pleasure of sharing their great knowledge with you as well.

Setting the right mood for any party includes pulling the five senses together in a way that is both simple yet savvy. But for many reluctant entertainers, pulling these five senses together can be intimidating. They have seen too many shows about entertaining or too many magazine spreads that make dinner table arrangements look like they came from a Hollywood set. They feel it's too steep a hill to climb to try to set the right mood for the evening, so many give up before even trying.

How exactly do we create a mood that completes our senses—sight, sound, taste, smell, and touch? I had a party recently that incorporated all five senses. It was an outdoor party, but the same principles apply to indoor parties as well.

VISUAL INSPIRATION

We all enjoy seeing beautiful things. One of the best ways to incorporate visual inspiration for your guests is to start at your front door. Your entry area is where guests receive their first impression of your home. It's important not to over-clutter it; making it beautiful and welcoming is easy enough through adding a seasonal wreath or some potted plants—something simple that says *Welcome*. The sense of sight can also be engaged through your table, flowers, and lighting.

For our outdoor dinner, the natural outside beauty was my décor for the evening, removing much of the decorating pressure. We took our guests out to the back patio area, where they could enjoy appetizers and see the attractive table setting. My standard white dishes, along with yellow cloth napkins, stood out against a gray tablecloth, an old standby I've used for years. Almost anything goes with gray! Two low-profile vases each held an iris, and two tea lights were ready to be lit at dusk. Color and order are appealing, so even though my chairs were mismatched, the simple yet attractive table is what grabbed people visually.

Adding fresh flowers is another excellent way to increase the visual appeal. We use what's blooming in our yard, but if that's not an option for you, grocery stores and farmers' markets offer good selections of fresh flowers. You might even consider asking a neighbor with a green thumb for a cutting from their garden.

Centerpieces add another layer of visual interest, but they do not have to be elaborate or fussy. I've learned the hard way that a centerpiece can be distracting if guests have to constantly look around it to see the person across the table. Use low-profile vases or different-sized canning jars for a fresh look.

Mix and match your plates, glasses, tables, and chairs, as long as there is a unifying theme.

Lighting sets the mood for many parties. If the lighting in your home is dull and dreary, the night usually comes off that way. What's needed is ambient light—it's warm and soft and creates a cozy feel. And the great news is that it's very inexpensive to achieve.

Candles are a great way to create ambient lighting. So is dimming your dining room lights. For an even more intimate setting, use low-lying tea lights indoors or out. During this particular evening, we lined our back patio with garden torches—which held citronella to ward off the mosquitoes.

Years ago we brought a fairy-tale flair to our backyard by hanging strings of white lights, offset by a few strings of orange lights, from our fence. It resulted in a magnificent, magical illumination. To our surprise, the orange lights actually go with any season. Such lighting can be intertwined throughout shrubs and trees, and they can be used indoors just as

Mouthwatering Sweet Steaks

Cousin Reggie's Marinade

1 clove garlic, minced
2 T. ketchup
1 T. balsamic vinegar
¼ cup soy sauce
¼ cup honey

Combine ingredients and pour into a zipper bag. Add steaks (or fillets) and marinate in refrigerator 24 to 48 hours. Cook as desired.

Variation: This marinade is also yummy with chicken.

Cousin Jim's St. Louis–Style Steaks

olive oil
sugar
seasoned salt (I use Lawry's)

Tenderize steaks with a mallet. Rub both sides of meat with olive oil, then sprinkle both sides with sugar and seasoned salt. Cook as desired.

effectively. Take advantage of post-holiday sales to pick up lights at substantial savings. I recommend LED lights, which are a little more expensive but last much longer. (Be sure lights are marked for outdoor use if that's where you'll be using them.)

SOUND CHECK

What people hear helps your evening to be even more enjoyable and memorable. Ideally, this begins when people come to your front door—or in our case, come through our side gate and into our backyard. We like to have music playing before people show up. Here's a tip that Paul learned as a waiter in college: Play your music a little louder than you normally would. This actually encourages more robust and spirited conversation because people will feel the need to compete with your music. Just be sure not to play it so loud that it completely dominates the airwaves, and be mindful of guests with hearing aids, who may need you to turn the music down.

Music that stimulates conversation can also help your shy guests talk more than usual, fostering more connection. And with more conversation comes more laughter, something everyone enjoys.

Music lightens the mood and acts as a kind of background icebreaker. It's one of the best tools you can have for creating a soothing atmosphere for your guests.

What kind of music should you use? This depends on what you enjoy as well as what works well for group settings. Generally speaking, music without lyrics works better because it tends to demand less from a person's ear. Most of the time we play instrumental jazz and soul with some verve to it. Then when people settle down for the meal, we will change the music to a more understated jazz or melodic classical. Mix your music up! Play some livelier tunes, followed by a slower piece of music, creating a kind of pleasant tension and release. This is what DJs are trained to do.

These days the Internet is a great source for free musical entertainment. We use Pandora.com, which allows you to create your own radio station around a single song or artist you like. Other free or low-cost Internet services include Rhapsody, Napster, Radio Tower, and Jukebox Alive.

If you have a child who plays a musical instrument, consider asking him or her to play for everyone after dinner. It doesn't really matter how accomplished the child is because adults often

enjoy it regardless. And for the child, it's good experience playing in front of a live audience—it builds courage and confidence. We like to include our guests' kids too, and give them a heads-up to come prepared. Our daughter, Abby, has played at many dinner parties, which has built her confidence to play in front of hundreds of people at a time. And lately she's been playing duets with our son Elliot on the piano.

Other sounds to incorporate—instead of trying to counteract them—are the sounds of children playing, whether inside or out in the backyard. If you have the space for outdoor games, set up a badminton or croquet set for the kids to enjoy. One of the older kids can be designated to supervise in order to keep things moving and to reduce possible conflicts. Or choose a movie for all of the kids to watch. When Paul and I were first married, we lived in a house of about nine hundred square feet. I remember sitting around the small dining room table visiting with our friends while all the kids piled on our bed in our bedroom to watch a movie. The brief humming of the TV—signaling contentment from the kids—spurred on the adult conversation we craved.

YUMMY SMELLS

Where we live, we're blessed to enjoy four distinct seasons, each bringing their own wonderful scents to relish. And smells can definitely trigger powerful memories. To this day, the smell of a roast in the oven reminds me of family Sunday dinners after church when I was growing up.

The mixed aromas of coals in the barbecue and citronella burning in the torch lanterns the night of our outdoor party are distinct in my mind.

Delicious smells can be powerful memory triggers for your guests as well. Welcome them with the whiff of warm appetizers or dessert just coming out of the oven. Fresh herbs can permeate your home with a sense of comfort and peace. I like to incorporate herbs into my table setting and in my main dishes. I think rosemary offers the biggest entitling bang, and I appreciate the reminder that rosemary is the symbol of friendship.

Years ago my husband and I enjoyed a great dinner with my Aunt Ellen in Toronto, where we were served olive oil infused with sea salt and fresh rosemary to go with our French bread. We have brought this simple bread dip to our guests, and the smell of the rosemary is one of the things our guests enjoy the most. We sometimes include homegrown cilantro in this dip as well, which is also full of great aroma.

Most of us can recall a memory with a smell, so why not let your house be one of them?

DISTINGUISHED TASTES

Taste is a sense that breaks down the walls of discomfort by bringing comfort. Even when the flavor might not be perfect, eating binds and soothes and settles us. Balancing the components of a meal can be fun, especially when you consider the color, the temperature, and even the textures, from smooth to crunchy. Keep in mind appetizers, salad, bread, main dish, and dessert when planning, although you don't have to be married to all of these courses. I like to take the first recipe that comes to mind, then build a menu around that, according to the season and what is growing in our garden. I almost always include a salad in my menu, no matter the season, because it's vibrant in color, and it's healthy!

For our summer evening party, I did not want to be a harried hostess, frantic in the kitchen and missing out on quality time with our guests. I wanted to serve something I could prepare in advance and that would also be simple for my husband, who does all of the barbecuing. I went with tri-tip steak, using an old standby marinade I could prepare a few days prior. It's always a crowd-pleaser, and I could already smell the meat on the grill.

We also try to cook at least one thing from our garden. Homegrown produce almost always tastes better than store bought, and there is a certain novelty to homegrown food that guests find appealing. For this evening we grilled homegrown potatoes and made a salad with our own lettuce. Surprisingly, the biggest hit of the evening wasn't the steak but the salad. I have to say it created quite the conversation.

Millie's Homemade Ice Cream

For generations now, my family has welcomed summer by making homemade ice cream. My dad and my grandpa took turns cranking the handle while we girls took turns sitting on the cold machine. This yummy vanilla homemade goodness is my mom's recipe, and it's a tradition I don't want to stop! Serves 10 to 12.

3 eggs, beaten
1 quart half-and-half cream
1 quart whipping cream
¾ cup white sugar
¾ cup brown sugar
1 tsp. salt
2¼ T. vanilla

In an extra large bowl, beat all the ingredients together. Pour into the ice cream freezer container for processing. Follow the instruction book for the freezer in layering the ice and rock salt.

Easy serving options:

- *Top with 3 T. hot espresso or strong coffee*

- *Serve with pound cake, white chocolate (Ghirardelli is my favorite), and fresh fruit*

- *Top with brownie chunks (pre-made in freezer) and chocolate sauce*

- *Layer in pretty glasses, alternating the ice cream with fruit, sauce, and brownies*

- *Serve with a quarter of cantaloupe*

We also served fresh bread one of our guests brought. A dessert of homemade vanilla ice cream with fresh berries and white chocolate sauce topped our night off perfectly. Some of the berries were strawberries from our backyard garden, which are easy to grow and taste so much better than what you get in the store.

FEELING THE TOUCH

Touch is perhaps the most forgotten sense when it comes to entertaining and hospitality. One area where we can bring touch into our events is with table linens. The feel of a starched tablecloth or even cotton napkins at an old picnic table makes one feel special. Even paper napkins, which I use a lot in the summertime, can introduce a fresh, crisp texture to the experience.

I wholeheartedly believe that glass feels better in a person's hand than paper or plastic, which is why I invested in my one-dollar water goblets. My guests feel special that I'm making extra effort in getting the "good" glasses out.

I realize that not all people are touchy-feely. But everyone is capable of giving a hug. Give your guests a hug when they walk through the front door or as they are leaving. Most people like to be touched in some small way. This particular summer party we had no problem being warm with one another. Even with a more reserved person, I find that when I put my arm around them, I can actually feel their body melt a bit.

The warmth of a fire can enhance the sense of touch as well. If you're entertaining outside, a fire pit or an outdoor fireplace can be a great social focal point. Not only does it help ward off the chill from the evening, but we've found that intimate conversation takes place around a fire and people relax and let their guard down. An indoor fireplace can draw guests out of the corners and into a warm circle of companionship.

For your next get-together, consider how you can engage all five senses. I guarantee you'll be surprised by how it helps you plan out your event. Preparation is the key, and thinking of the "five" will prevent the gathering from being boring, sterile, and cold. It signals to your guests that they are worth a little extra effort and that they are loved.

The Heart of Hospitality: Conversation

During a recent overnight trip to a cabin with some friends, we went on a three-hour hike around the lake. The seven of us stopped halfway around the lake for a snack of dried veggies, nuts, cookies, and water. We sat on stumps and on the ground and enjoyed taking in the beautiful late-summer day.

As we sat there, enjoying a light breeze coming off the small lake, I noticed that our conversation took on a deeper tone. It wasn't somber, but it went toward more meaningful topics like friendships that end and then come back. Or kids who worry us but then somehow seem to straighten out on their own. This wasn't how our conversations flowed while we were hiking, and I realized that one reason for this deeper conversation was that we were now sharing a meal. It's a simple difference, but when it comes to conversation, it makes a world of difference. There's something about food that draws us together and opens us up. Edith Schaeffer, in *The Hidden Art of Homemaking*, puts it this way:

> *Food and meal-times shared have always been thought of as a closer kind of communication than simply talking to people, without eating together. The very sharing of a short break to*

drink a cup of tea, a glass of juice or a cup of coffee together, is in itself a kind of communication.

Food, conversation, and connection go hand in hand, don't they? But for most of us, eating food comes naturally—it's the conversation part that can be pretty hard.

According to most of the people who contact me through my blog, conversation doesn't come easy for many people. It didn't always come easy in our home when my husband and I were newly married and I wanted to entertain. I was an eager young hostess ready to use the hospitality skills I had learned so well from my parents, but I realized there was one hang-up: My husband wasn't as eager as I was! You could say he was my original reluctant entertainer. His dragging his feet had a lot to do with conversation. Like a lot of guys, my husband wasn't a conversationalist—certainly not the one he is today! I took his reluctance personally, and I thought, *You've got to be kidding me! I've waited all these years to entertain, and now you're telling me my husband's just not into it?*

Everyone has a story, and people like to be heard. Have a question ready to ask your guests in the first few minutes of your meal together.

During those early years in our marriage, my husband became proactive, realizing that my love for entertaining wouldn't go away. Although he was private about it, he picked up a small book on conversation starters. He first started using it on our date nights, asking me new questions each week. As he grew more comfortable, he began bringing similar questions to the table to use with our guests. I look back now and think, *What a guy. I can't believe he would do that for me!*

We learned together the concept of planning out the conversation, to talk ahead of time about what question we'd start our dinner with. Once we mastered that, the art of conversation became easier, and it eventually evolved and became richer and richer.

One of the most common questions I receive about conversations is, "Where do I start?" Instead of providing primer questions (we'll get to those later), I encourage people to take a certain philosophical approach toward others, which goes to the heart of hospitality. To become better conversationalists, it's important that we cultivate a genuine curiosity toward others. Everyone has remarkable stories inside of them—it's the job of a good conversationalist and hostess to help them bring that story out.

Sometimes people are afraid to go this deep. Going deep takes courage, and courage means following something more important than our own fears. It can be hard at first, but soon you'll experience how people feel cared for when you ask questions about their life.

Here are some easy conversation starters that will help your next gathering be more meaningful and hospitable than it might be otherwise:

- Who made you feel best about yourself as a child and why?
- Who's your hero, or someone you admire?
- What day would you love to live over again?

DIVINE QUESTIONS

One night my husband and I invited six guests over, and this time I left it up to my husband to come up with two fun, preplanned questions to help us all get to know one another better. We believe a divine intervention took place that evening.

The eight of us were enjoying the night with much laughter, when my husband directed the conversation by asking: "What is your middle name and why was it given to you?" Then, "If you went to college, what is your degree in?"

Little did we know that our single friend's date had vowed that he would never discuss either question! Our single girlfriend's jaw dropped when my husband asked these two simple questions because she knew that it appeared to be a setup. Amazingly, though, Paul had never discussed these with anyone, not even me, and certainly not our friend. This was so outside the realm of possibility, so unusual, that we believe it was actually divine, because it revealed a portion of that man's nature that was a very bad fit for our single friend. All of us, not just Paul and I, knew that this man was not the one for our friend. By asking the right questions, sometimes we find out about the wrong person!

Another cold winter's weeknight we were invited to our friend Jenny's house for a casual dinner. I so appreciate casual and last-minute invitations because people are just looking for connection, and I enjoy any kind of invitation, even on a weeknight.

Jenny is a nurse and a very hard worker, and I was so impressed that she and her husband would even consider having four of us over during the week. But Jenny isn't tripped up by the illusion of perfection, and this night she hosted a very simple get-together. She planned the Mexican buffet ahead of time, cooking my easy chicken mango recipe in the slow cooker all day and preparing the toppings the night before. One couple brought the chips and guacamole; I brought dessert.

The six of us thought we knew each other pretty well, but the conversation went even richer that night due to a simple but potent question: What is your favorite childhood memory?

Interestingly, the answer for most around the table was camping. We shared funny stories, personal stories, stories about our parents—experiences all very unique, forming and molding each of us into who we are today. We really learned a lot about our pasts and gained a new appreciation for one another, all by sharing one simple question that got the group on the same subject and sharing intimate memories.

Deeper questions have their place, but not with every gathering. Here are some other questions that will help your guests get to know each other while staying on the lighter but still meaningful side of life:

- Share a memory of a teacher or a coach who impacted you as a child.

- If you had to move to a new place, where would that be?

- If you could trade houses with someone for two weeks, whose house would you choose?

- What's your favorite memory of someone in this room? (This is perfect for guests who know each other.)

- What's one of the most memorable things you've done in your lifetime?

• What is something that you learned from your grandparents or an older relative?

We've discovered something remarkable about asking both deeper and lighter conversation starters: There is always laughter and there are sometimes tears as well. It's not because someone is hurt but because they remember something that hurt—but remembering it in the company of people who accept them, like them, and even love them.

An easy conversation starter that includes children is a question we ask at our dinner table almost every night: "What was the best and worst part of your day?" We often ask our kids' friends the same question when they join us in a meal. Sometimes we take it a bit further: "Share about a person in your life who builds you up." Or "What is one of the most adventurous things you've ever done?"

We find that respect for each other grows after these questions are asked and answered, especially when a parent at the table enforces the rule that each person deserves to be listened to with full interest and should not be interrupted while speaking.

THE PENNY GAME

This fun conversation starter involves rounding up pennies with dates that roughly correspond with the childhood (and beyond) years of your guests. The hostess selects a penny for each guest and places it under the water goblet where that person will sit. For example, someone born in 1963 should get a penny from about 1968 or later. Once dinner begins, each guest takes their turn looking at the date on their penny and sharing something significant about their life from that year. You can change it up at the last minute and say the penny under each glass is for the person on their right or left. That really throws a spin on the game. The stories can range from guests' younger years in life to the most recent. It's a fun way to learn something new about each other.

CONVERSATION FOR ALL

As a younger hostess I'd sometimes feel disappointment in the end result of some of my dinner parties. There was a *lack of soul*. I went to my husband and asked him to help me figure out why, and we discovered a pattern. It was usually the result of one person being allowed to dominate the entire conversation, or one "sour grape" putting a negative spin on the whole evening. It was distracting and it took the place of what could have been a more meaningful time.

We decided to look into this idea more, and it steered us into reading up on conversation. We learned the importance of including everyone around the table, and that it was the respon-  sibility of the hosts. Yikes, that was us! We learned through a couple of bad experiences, where we unknowingly allowed this to happen, that we needed to take charge without appear- ing rude. We had a new goal in mind: to make the conversation and dinnertime as soulful as possible for all.

A few years ago, when my family was new to the neighborhood, I decided to host a salad luncheon for twelve neighbor ladies, who ranged in age from ten to seventy-five. I did not care about impressing, but rather I wanted to experience connection among my neighbors.

My daughter and I hand-delivered the invi- tations, meeting each neighbor face-to-face— which I believe had something to do with our good turnout. Almost all of the ladies invited were able to come. By this time I had learned the importance of taking charge and starting the conversation, and I asked these simple questions: "Where were you born?" "How many years have you lived in your current home?" "What is the history behind the home you live in?" Each lady got to share something about herself and her history, and what brought her to the neighborhood, which is what we all shared in common.

One thing I've learned about parties is that you can never re-create the same exact party. So the next year I added a few new faces. But I do have one confession. There was one lady I did not invite back because of her dominating, rude personality. During that first luncheon, one older, wiser neighbor stepped up and graciously helped move the conversation on. Shirley and I had made eye contact, and we both knew something needed to be done before the conversation went bad.

Having intentional conversation and steering it in a positive direction is something that we as hosts can learn. When you mix different personalities, you sometimes have to be aware and be willing to change the direction of conversation. Sometimes there is one bad apple in the group, and it's up to us to not let one person spoil the time for others. There needs to be an appropriate amount of grace and freedom in order to bring people out of isolation—in this case elderly neighbors—and back into the community, where health grows. I decided

Asking specific questions gives each guest a chance to share and not be overshadowed by others.

that this one person would not be allowed to dominate one of my parties again. This didn't make her a bad person, just an inappropriate person for what I was trying to accomplish.

A few summers back I held a dinner party in my backyard for some women friends. I asked a simple question that would break the ice and help us learn more about each other: "What is new in your life, something that none of us at this table might be aware of?"

As we went around the table that glorious summer night, some went deeper than others, but it was beautiful to witness the passions and gifts that were flowing from each individual. We all benefited from seeing each other's recent accomplishments or current tasks at hand. I think we ladies learned that night how to recognize and

Slow Cooker Chicken or Pork

Both of these recipes are excellent for tacos, taco salad, enchiladas, or burritos. You can even use the leftovers in chili. Mango salsa happens to be one of our family favorites. The pork inspiration came from my friend Kristi. Serves 8 to 10.

Chicken:
3 lbs. boneless, skinless chicken breasts, seasoned with salt and pepper
2 cups mango salsa (any salsa works)

Pork:
2 small picnic pork roasts (frozen works great!)
1 can cream of chicken soup
1 small can green chiles

Spray inside of slow cooker with nonstick cooking spray. Place meat in the crock and cover with salsa (chicken) or soup and chiles (pork). Cook on low 8 hours. Do not stir. Before serving, shred the meat with two forks. (Do not drain the chicken; it will absorb the juices.)

affirm what may not be obvious on the outside. We instead saw the hidden qualities that make an individual a person of worth and dignity.

After the dinner, a more reserved friend commented on how special the "question" part of the evening was for her. She admitted that, as the quietest person in the group, she often feels insignificant and out of the conversation when a dominating person takes center stage. There always seems to be one of those in a group, I'd say. But this particular night was different for her because every woman had a chance to voice her story.

RESERVED HOSTS

Some hosts just have a hard time getting conversations started. I've heard numerous stories from women who have tried hosting parties but it didn't go well, so they've given up on entertaining completely. And almost always it's not the meal that failed them—it's the conversation.

If you're not the kind of host who likes to lead a conversation, that's okay. Before the party gets going, quietly ask a naturally outspoken person to pose creative conversation starters. Then watch how that person does it to learn how you can do the same someday.

Or consider creative assigned seating. Think ahead about who could benefit from sitting by whom—you might put a shy person next to a more outgoing person. If one of the guests tends to dominate the conversation, put them next to you or next to another strong personality. The goal isn't to shut the person down but to simply manage them.

If my party has more than six people—and if I have the time—I love to use place cards at my table settings. Conversation just comes alive when you can mix up the group. When my daughter was younger, she'd create the cards. A child's touch takes the pressure off of perfection for sure, and it also gets the child involved in hospitality in a meaningful way.

Our family was once invited to a dinner party that has since become a fond memory for all of us. The hostess sat each younger person next to an older person. It was a night that our kids talked about for a long time, and I really appreciate the effort our hosts put into planning the conversation around fourteen people. Our kids can learn from older and wiser adults, and we know that our older friends find kids unique and intriguing.

Our goal is to never have cookie-cutter talk—always the same, always safe, and sometimes boring. At one dinner party of ours, the conversation revolved around the virtue of courage. We wanted to mix it up and give everyone the chance to speak the language of love and courage, to uplift and bolster one another in our walks in life. Five hours later, we were still engaging in the battle of standing up for what is right in this world, no matter what the cost. Bodies leaned forward, voices rose in passion, tears were shed, and our hearts were

very open to the spirit moving. Sometimes we don't always know what we're missing until we experience something really wonderful.

The heart of hospitality is where people feel loved, cherished, and valuable. And more times than not, the bridge to hospitality is paved with words that come from meaningful questions and attuned ears. And around the table, sharing food is where it usually happens.

Take the time

Ask the right questions

Break bread

Listen

Empathize

Mexican Flan Cake

This recipe is revised from my days as a Pampered Chef consultant years ago. I made this in so many kitchens—it wowed my guests every time and feeds a crowd! Serves 12.

1 cup sugar
½ cup water
1½ cups milk (not skim)
8 egg yolks
1 can (14 oz.) sweetened
    condensed milk
2 tsp. orange zest
2 tsp. vanilla
1 tsp. cinnamon
1 pkg. (16 oz.) pound cake mix
¼ cup milk (not skim)
¼ cup orange juice
2 eggs

Spray an 11-inch round baking pan with nonstick cooking spray. Combine sugar and water in a medium saucepan. While stirring to dissolve the sugar, bring to a full boil over medium-high heat. Reduce heat to medium low; let cook 20 to 25 minutes, until sugar turns golden brown and caramelizes. Do not stir. Quickly pour caramelized sugar mixture into baking pan, tilting to evenly cover the bottom of the pan with the glaze. Set aside.

Preheat oven to 375°F.

In a medium bowl whisk together 1½ cups milk, egg yolks, condensed milk, orange zest, vanilla, and cinnamon until well blended. Pour over the caramelized sugar mixture in the pan.

In a medium bowl combine cake mix, ¼ cup milk, orange juice, and eggs and mix well. Spoon batter evenly over the custard mixture.

Bake 30 to 35 minutes or until cake springs back when touched lightly in center. Cool 20 minutes. Loosen edge with knife. Invert dessert onto a large heat-resistant serving plate.

Serve warm or cool. Store leftover dessert covered in the refrigerator.

More Than Dinner Parties: Deeper Connections

When I think of hospitality, it goes far beyond the standard dinner party. Hospitality happens in our homes, in our churches, and in our neighborhoods. It's the spark of friendships, of soul-satisfying experiences with others, eventually taking us to deeper connections as we learn how to reach out.

One cool spring evening, my husband and I drove less than a mile up the road to one of our favorite restaurants, Bambu. It was date night for us, something we prioritized early in our marriage. The brisk spring air was too chilly for sitting out on the patio, so we chose a small table inside. On both sides of us sat older couples. We began a conversation with the couple to our left, and then with the couple to our right, and at one point all six of us were talking together.

Afterward I pointed out to my husband why we enjoy older people so much. They're easy to talk to, they're interested in our lives, and they're just more relaxed. My husband, on the other hand, expressed his theory, which has been proven over and over in our marriage: Older people have nothing to prove, so they are sometimes more authentic and enjoyable.

They've lived most of their lives, climbed the ladders of their careers. They've raised their children, and most are now grandparents. They just don't talk about themselves as much, the way younger people tend to do. They are not interested in comparing their lives. Instead they share their lives, and none claim to be experts about everything. They tend to be much better listeners, and all of this helps them forge deeper and more genuine relationships.

INVEST IN OLDER FRIENDSHIPS

Paul and I have had a yearly tradition of entertaining two older couples. Not only have these couples invested their time and energy into sharing meals with us, but they have attended our children's musical events, sporting events, and school activities; they have given financial support for mission trips; and they have shared with us loads of blessings from their gardens and orchard. One night as they were leaving our house, one of the ladies said, "You know, we rarely get invited over to young couples' homes anymore."

It's by sharing our stories and our lives—the good, bad, glorious, and ugly—that we become knowable to others.

Her simple statement hit me hard. Our generation would be healthier and so much happier if we could see the value in practicing hospitality outside of our age group. Often we forget that we are as much a gift to others as they are to us.

Howard was a similar gift in our lives, and if I hadn't slowed down about five years ago, I would have missed out on a beautiful relationship with my ninety-eight-year-old neighbor.

Howard lived at the end of our street. All we knew about Howard was that he lived in the pink-and-brown house, he drove a golf cart, and he'd give a quick wave every night at about six as he headed up to the country club for dinner. It was through our son's summer watering job that we finally met Howard, and our life was changed. As his body started declining, I started helping him out more and more. He was no longer able to cook for himself, and I found myself taking dinner to him every Monday night, when the country club was closed.

What I cooked for my family, I'd dish up smaller portions for Howard, and always included my home-canned fruit, which he loved. Sometimes my kids joined me in delivering the tray of food down the street to his home.

Howard would often ask me, as I drove him around to run errands and pick up his medicines, "Sandy, why are you so kind to me?" He was struggling with the thought that someday he might have to move into an assisted living home. I gave him the same answer every time: "Howard, I am an angel in your life." I didn't have an agenda, except to reach out and help someone in need. And it was evident that I was the person to do this. The gift of food was a blessing to Howard, and in receiving it, he was a blessing to us.

Our older friends have shown me that the soul of entertaining and hospitality isn't about putting on a great dinner party, fun as that is. Though great connections happen during these times, our older friends have taught me a profound truth: Some of the best ways to express hospitality take place outside our dining rooms and backyard patio sets.

Hoppi showed me this as well.

For almost two years, on Thursday nights our family was the recipient of an amazing home-cooked meal delivered to our house by Hoppi, a former neighbor. Hoppi decided to take her talents (as a natural gourmet cook) and bless our family with a healthy meal on a night that would help us out the most. It was perfect timing for our family during the busiest season of our lives. My children came to love and appreciate this generous woman, learning a great life lesson from her determination to reach out and bless us. I believe that when our children are grown, they will do for others what we did for Howard and what Hoppi did for us.

HOSPITALITY ON WHEELS

Hospitality covers the whole range of life experiences and emotions. For me, some of those life experiences and emotions have come in challenging times, like when I had each of my three kids, when my mother died, and two different occasions when I had surgery. Friends rallied together and brought our family meals, and we were very blessed.

Taking meals to those in need is often a ministry in churches. But it shouldn't just be church friends we look out for. Our world is full of need. Here are five simple steps to putting hospitality on wheels:

1. Call and ask if the family would like to receive a meal.
2. Make sure the family knows when you will be delivering the meal.
3. Keep the meal simple, whether it is one entrée or a full course.
4. If possible, use disposable dishes so the recipient doesn't have to worry about washing dishes and getting them back to you.
5. Don't plan to stay and visit unless you are invited in.

If you know a family is going to need help for an extended period of time, setting up a meal schedule can be a huge blessing. Here are some simple steps to playing this role:

1. Ask the family if they'd like to receive meals, and then ask for names of some close friends, neighbors, or family members.
2. Ask when the family would like the first meal, and for how long the meals should continue. (I usually plan two weeks for a surgery, and sometimes up to three weeks for a new birth.) Let them know to expect a meal every other day, and decide with them on a set time when the meals should be delivered.
3. Set up a calendar, or make your own on a blank piece of paper.
4. When you make your calls, it's not important to know each person's contribution. It puts pressure on the cook to decide right then (and she may feel locked in).
5. Fill in the calendar for the full duration, including names and phone numbers of those making the meals. Then mail or email the recipients the information.

Once the schedule is sent, my mission is accomplished. The family is on their way to being blessed and there's really nothing more I plan to do. I never "baby-sit" the schedule. I just let it flow and happen on its own. Yes, there are times when someone will forget to take the meal, but the receiving family has the schedule with phone numbers.

My favorite meal to take is whatever I happen to be cooking for dinner that night. It's easy to just double up on ingredients and make two batches instead of one. Other easy and "portable" meals people tend to enjoy include enchiladas, a roasted chicken with salad in a bag, pizza, potpie, spaghetti, and even frozen lasagna.

Again, hospitality, like life, can be messy and imperfect. It doesn't matter if a family gets the same meal two nights in a row—most families are very thankful for whatever food is brought. When I had foot surgery, we received enchiladas two nights in a row. We didn't care! Another night that week friends stopped by unannounced, and we put the second pan of enchiladas to good use along with a quick tossed salad. It was an odd feeling for me, being laid up on the back patio while my friend Myrna rummaged through my kitchen putting the meal together. But I actually enjoyed the feeling of watching other people being hospitable in my own home. And thanks to my sister Linda's hospitable spirit in bringing me a meal, we were able to enjoy a spontaneous meal with friends.

Another creative form of hospitality is swapping a meal with another family once a week. You cook for their family, and they cook for yours. My family loves the variety we get through this meal swap. Some of my kids' friends' moms are their favorite cooks! Go a step further and save time and energy by making two of the same meal—take one to the other family and save the second for your family to eat the next night.

DROP AND RUN MEALS

Most women have a servant's heart. They want to do something, but they aren't sure where to start or what to do. If you have school-age children, why not start with one of their teachers? A few years ago I recruited a group of moms to take turns preparing dinner for our children's fifth-grade teacher, Mrs. Peterson. Twice a month during the school year, one of us "invisible moms" slips in at the end of the day to drop off a meal for this hardworking teacher and her family. She knows it's coming (we cleared it with her in advance), but she doesn't necessarily know who's bringing it.

After several weeks of receiving meals, Mrs. Peterson pulled me aside at school and said, "The word is spreading. Teachers cannot believe that you moms would bring me and my family dinner!" She said that it was a huge blessing to her to have one meal a week that she didn't have to prepare or even think about. On those Wednesdays her family was able to sit down around the table and simply enjoy the evening together.

This form of hospitality is not daunting, and the commitment is not huge—it's something any mom can do.

1. Find five moms in your child's classroom who like to cook.
2. Set a schedule of once a week, or every other week, for the meal to be delivered (right before the teacher leaves at the end of the day).
3. Give the schedule to the teacher in advance, so she knows when she has the nights off from cooking.
4. Slip in, drop the meal off (use disposable pans), and leave.

In this case, Mrs. Peterson knew I was involved, but you can do it anonymously if you'd like.

Our family was the recipient of an anonymous blessing recently. The doorbell rang, and we opened the door to find a tray filled with muffins, cookies, and a beautiful cake, along with a card that simply said, *Because I have an oven.*

Our home was in chaos, due to a major kitchen remodel. We'd set up a makeshift kitchen in the garage, but we had no working ovens. That anonymous giver really knew how to make our family happy—by bringing treats! We were so blessed by someone seeing our need and filling it.

INSPIRING HOSPITALITY IN OUR CHILDREN

About five years ago I started a group for girls called the Balcony Girls. Opening my home to these girls was not only a way I could use my gifts, but it was also a way that I could teach my daughter to be hospitable.

A book I had read in my twenties, *Balcony People* by Joyce Landorf Heatherley, inspired me to bring eight girls to my home twice a month after school, to have fun with a lesson, craft, and snack.

Dill Bread

This is my friend Pam's specialty. You know you have a specialty when you're asked to bring the same thing to every dinner party! Serves 6.

1 pkg. dry yeast
½ cup warm water
1 cup cottage cheese,
    room temperature
2 T. sugar
¼ cup minced onions
1 T. butter, melted
2 T. dried dill
    or chopped fresh dill

1 tsp. salt
¼ tsp. baking soda
1 egg
2¼ cups all-purpose flour
melted butter
coarse salt

In a small bowl, pour yeast over warm water. Let stand for 5 minutes.

In a large mixing bowl, combine cottage cheese, sugar, onion, butter, dill, 1 tsp. salt, baking soda, egg, and yeast-water mixture. Add flour in portions, beating after each addition, to form a stiff ball. Cover bowl and let dough rise until doubled in size, about 1 hour.

Punch dough down and turn into well-greased 1½- to 2-quart ovenproof dish. Let dough rise another 30 to 40 minutes until light.

Preheat oven to 350°F. Bake for 40 to 45 minutes, until golden brown. Brush with butter and sprinkle with coarse salt.

My goal was to help them navigate through relationships, cliques, and bad situations, and to teach the concept of building others up and not tearing them down.

This group has taken focus and energy. But each time I see the fruits of what is taking place, I know I cannot give it up. It has eternal value that we may not see now but will be impacting and will help these girls as they grow. True hospitality is not always easy, and it's not always pretty—but it is about giving to others even when you're tired and you might not feel like it. I've felt that way many times, but I pushed through it and inspiration came.

Hospitality always starts with a spark of inspiration. Once it's ignited, we can enjoy watching the flame grow and even perhaps spark more inspiration in others.

PROGRESSIVE NIGHT

In chapter 5 I listed many types of parties or gatherings you could hold in your home. One tradition my husband and I have enjoyed the past five years at Christmastime is a progressive dinner, where the party literally picks up and moves from place to place throughout the evening. In our case, it's four courses in four homes. We plan a meal together and divide up the courses to be served at a different participant's home. It's a great way to take the reluctance out of entertaining when all you have to provide is one course. And it's a great way to connect with new or old friends. We look forward to this evening all year.

Deeper connections come from years of friendships, and for some of us in this group, the connection goes back thirty years. Our families have all felt life at its hardest and joy at its fullest. We've experienced death, divorce, blended families, caring for elderly parents, adoption, job losses, and parenting challenges. We've had many celebrations along the way too. One year the last home was under construction for a kitchen remodel, but you never would have known it. As we walked in the front doors, Cindy's house was so warm and inviting; the ambience and background music made Christmas come alive. It was again another lesson for me to let go of imperfection and to welcome love, which comes pretty easily with this group of friends.

What matters in the end is that we love. If you are reading this and have never experienced this deeper connection, it's not too late to start. Take the initiative and find a group of friends to start a progressive dinner, whether it's just another weeknight, a weekend date night, or even a holiday like Thanksgiving, Easter, or New Year's Day.

When we spend a few hours with a group, discovering each other's weaknesses and strengths, allowing ourselves to go deeper, to be vulnerable, we actually find ourselves loving others in a more passionate way.

PROGRESSIVE DINNER

1. Find three or four couples or individuals with whom you share similar interests or who you think would be compatible sharing a whole evening together.
2. Make sure all parties (including yourselves) live within a short distance of one another (unless you don't mind driving a longer distance for one course).
3. Divide the courses up by appetizers, salad, main dish, and dessert (add in a soup course if there are five homes participating).
4. Set the time (we like to start as early as 4 p.m.) and date.
5. Allow one hour for most courses and an hour and a half for the main course.
6. If it's a hit, make it a tradition!

Carrot Orange Soup

I always double or even triple this recipe. It's great for a crowd and is delicious leftover. The recipe came from my friend Julie, who served it to Paul and me at a dinner party years ago. Serves 6.

4 T. butter
2 cups finely chopped yellow onions
    (I use sweet onions)
12 large carrots (1½ to 2 lbs.),
    peeled and chopped
4 cups chicken stock, divided
1 cup fresh orange juice
salt and freshly ground pepper, to taste
fresh grated orange zest, to taste

In a large saucepan or kettle, melt butter. Sauté onions on low heat for 25 minutes. Add carrots and half of the stock and bring to a boil. Reduce heat and simmer for 30 minutes. Blend the mixture in blender or food processor to the texture you prefer. Return to the pot and add the rest of the stock, orange juice, salt, pepper, and zest. Serve hot.

From Reluctant to Gracious Living

If there is one word that helps us move from being a reluctant entertainer to a more confident one, it's *grace*. Grace takes so much stress away and paves the way for what many of us long for today: a path from isolation to connection and deep friendships.

When I'm a guest in someone's home, I take to heart the hard work a hostess has put into her meal. I try to make light of situations that might be embarrassing to her, like if her kids act up. I know exactly what that is like, because my kids have acted up when I was entertaining. My children are older now, yet I still try to remember what it was like when life was more hectic and I had less experience as a hostess than I have now.

I realize how fortunate I have been when it comes to hostessing, because I had so many great role models in my life. My mother and her five sisters were incredible women. I admire how classy they were, and how gracious, kind, warm, courteous, and generous they were toward others. As a little girl I watched how well they focused on their guests' comfort and pleasure. In a very real way, this book is kind of like a baton that was handed to me by those gracious hostesses, which I'm now handing off to you.

nine

Becoming like them—those gracious hostesses—took many, many years, but I decided early on that graciousness is one of the most beautiful traits a person can have, and I wanted it for myself. It portrays contentment, which leads to a great attitude toward life. It's accepting how our life is today, with little or with much. It's learning to extend to others with a joyful heart a part of ourselves that could easily be thwarted if we gave in to the voices of perfection that diminish our lives, our homes, and our ability to create close connections with others.

The Bible sheds light on one of the secrets to gracious living:

I've learned by now to be quite content whatever my circumstances. I'm just as happy with little as with much, with much as with little. I've found the recipe for being happy whether full or hungry, hands full or hands empty. Whatever I have, wherever I am, I can make it through anything in the One who makes me who I am. (Philippians 4:10–14, THE MESSAGE)

Two things come to mind when I think of grace: God's unmerited favor, and a simple prayer we offer before we eat, especially when we share a meal with others. It says thank-you even when our situation might be hard and

far from perfect. And as I emphasized earlier in this book, when it comes to entertaining, there is no such thing as perfect.

I'm reminded of a family dinner recently, eaten while sitting in our living room because our kitchen was turned upside-down for remodeling. My husband said grace before we ate, and then I asked our kids why we call our prayers grace. Abby said, "It's when God gives us so much, we really want to thank Him."

PRACTICE GRACE

We can practice being gracious right in our own homes. Our houses don't have to be large or beautiful, and we don't even have to own them. No matter what our living arrangements are, we can practice grace by sharing our lives, experiences, and food with others with an attitude that says, "You are cared about exactly how you are." Being gracious in our homes means that we value being polite and respectful. When we extend these values to others, it's doubly good because they are returned back to us.

My Auntie Ellen—my dad's sister-in-law—was a great example of being a gracious hostess. She showed great interest in my life from the time I was five and would become an influential and gracious person throughout my life. She showed a genuine interest in me by forging deep relationships with my family and by being so gracious to us when we visited her in St. Louis.

Life wasn't always easy for her. She lost her husband—my dad's brother—at the young age of thirty-three, and raised their three children alone. But she wasn't really alone. All those years of being single, Aunt Ellen lived a gracious life by reaching out and loving friends, co-workers, and people throughout her community. She was a role model that many looked up to, eventually becoming St. Louis Business Woman of the Year. She was known for her generosity and gracious style, and our daughter, Abby, has the middle name of Ellen in honor of such a wonderful person.

I also think of all the other women who have inspired me—my mom, her sisters, my sisters, my many amazing cousins, my fabulous stepmom,

Leftovers Potpie With Cheesy Crust Topping

Good enough for company, every time! Serves 8.

Cheesy Crust Topping:

2 cups flour

¾ cup butter, chilled and cut into small pieces

1 cup shredded cheddar cheese

½ cup ice water

1 egg white, whipped

Filling:

4 cups leftover cooked chicken (rotisserie works great)

1 pkg. (16 oz.) frozen green peas and carrots

Parmesan sauce (recipe on p. 55)

any leftover cooked veggies in the fridge

any leftover cooked potatoes in the fridge

In a medium bowl, use a pastry blender (or fingertips) to work the butter into the flour until the mixture is crumbly. Add the cheese and work in until just blended. Sprinkle ice water over the pastry dough, a little at a time, and gather the pastry into a ball. Knead until just combined. Wrap in plastic wrap and chill in the refrigerator.

Cook the frozen peas and carrots as directed on the package and set aside. Prepare the white sauce and set aside.

Preheat oven to 375°F. Spray a 9" x 13" baking dish with nonstick cooking spray. Place the chicken in the baking dish. Layer the peas and carrots, leftover veggies, and leftover potatoes on top of the chicken. Pour hot Parmesan sauce over everything.

On a floured surface, roll out the chilled dough into a 9" x 13" rectangle. Place the pastry on your pie, and trim away any overhanging edges. Score with a knife and brush with egg white.

Bake 25 to 30 minutes, or until pastry is golden brown and filling is bubbly. Cool for 10 minutes before serving.

Option: As a shortcut for the crust, use a puff pastry sheet, 2 pkgs. of crescent rolls, or 2 pkgs. of refrigerated biscuits.

and many other women who've impacted my entertaining experiences. I know one thing: I'm attracted to and grateful for gracious people.

Auntie Ellen and I always appreciated how food brought people together. Every time we were together we would plan a party. Whether we were hanging out in the kitchen, shopping, or making a flower arrangement together, she taught me to enjoy what I was doing, to keep a good attitude, and to focus on the moment. She'd let me know that her kitchen was my kitchen, and she'd encourage me to be creative—then give me credit for the way it turned out, when in reality it was her brilliant idea. A nugget she taught me is that although food is important, it's not what makes entertaining successful. She taught me that what really matters is the grace you extend to those around your table, no matter what their background, religion, or beliefs. This approach removes rigidity and expectations and spreads sharing, loving, patience, and understanding—all attributes of a gracious lifestyle.

And more times than not, this gracious attitude shows itself at the dinner table, where people feel free to open up and share their joys as well as their struggles. We remember that God is gracious with us, so we should be gracious toward one another.

I was raised in a musical home, and we sang our family prayer before each meal when our large families got together. We'd harmonize and sing with slow, heartfelt words that reminded us of God's love for us:

God is great and God is good.
And we thank Him for our food.
By His hand must all be fed.
Give us, Lord, our daily bread.
Amen.

I think of my friend Liz Curtis Higgs, who says in her book *Embrace Grace* that there's enough grace for each of us, for everyone we love, and for the whole planet. She says, "Resist the urge to complicate [grace]. Keep the image of a gift firmly in mind. A present you can give to others. Freely. Gladly."

Grace is a gift I both give and receive. A great example is from one particular night when our friends from Reno stopped in for a quick visit, which turned into dinner. I was already making the meal, so I asked them to stay. We caught up with their lovely family and together we enjoyed a meal of chicken potpie with a cheesy crust on top. I was relaxed and spontaneous that night, which took the pressure off my family (who don't really care if things are perfect). And it was a huge gift to our friends, saying to them that I was willing to drop everything, open our doors— mess and all—and invite them in. It said that they were more important than what they might think of me and us.

Food brings us to the table, but it is grace, the soft and golden butter on the warm bread of the common life, that makes us want to stay there.

Hootenanny

My Aunt Ellen served this breakfast dish every time I visited her in St. Louis. It's great for company, and you can even double up the recipe if you have a crowd to feed. Serves 6.

6 eggs
1 cup milk
½ tsp. salt
1 cup flour
¼ cup butter, melted
powdered sugar
fresh squeezed lemon juice
maple syrup (optional)

Preheat oven to 425°F.

Combine eggs, milk, and salt in a blender. Blend until fluffy. Add flour a little at a time until blended.

Pour melted butter into a 9" x 13" baking dish. Pour the egg batter into the baking dish. Bake for 18 minutes.

Cut into squares. Serve sprinkled with powdered sugar and fresh squeezed lemon juice. Serve with maple syrup if desired.

Pantry Talk

Pantries can take on a variety of shapes and sizes, depending on the space your kitchen affords you. It could be anything from a single kitchen cupboard to a freestanding hutch to a spacious walk-in pantry—or even some dedicated shelves in the garage, like I used for years before our kitchen remodel.

The secret to an effective pantry, whether it's large or small, is keeping it organized. Because let me tell you, it defeats the whole purpose of being "prepared" when you let your pantry get out of control. I cringe over the amount of food I have tossed because it was stale or expired after being shoved to the back of the cupboard—usually when I was in a hurry and wasn't working to keep my pantry area organized. Rotating your items is an important part of pantry organization. When new food comes home from the store, place it behind the food already on the shelf so you use up the old first.

Having a well-stocked pantry, fridge, and freezer can also provide a sense of security, efficiency, and control. The more I attempt to develop an organized plan for my pantry, the better I become with meal planning and last-minute dishes to suit the day. Not only do I know my family will be fed, but I also have the supplies to pull a meal together if unexpected guests should pop in.

In chapter 4 I talked about having a few signature dishes to make when you entertain. It's a good idea to always be stocked up with the ingredients for those dishes so you can make one in a hurry if needed. My old standby recipes are green enchiladas, spicy chicken chili, curry chicken and rice, and for dessert cherry crunch—and I try to always have their ingredients on hand.

A stocked pantry also helps me teach my kids to be resourceful. When I hear, "Mom, there's no food in the house," I can point them to the pantry to find something to eat. Having food stocked also keeps us away from eating fast food (eating at home is always the healthy route to take), or running to the store at the last minute.

Organization is far more important than just stocking up with a lot of food. My mom was not much of a stocker-upper. She was organized, did her once-a-week shopping, and never ran back to the store on a whim. Having an organized system saved her time and money. She planned meals and any entertaining she'd do for the upcoming week and then made her grocery list. On Saturday morning she headed to the grocery store with one of us girls. We didn't have warehouse clubs or discount groceries back then, and my mom was not excessive in her shopping, but I learned a lot from her.

REORGANIZE AND RESTOCK

When you're ready to take control of your pantry, start by looking at your space. Can you easily find what you need? Are like items grouped together? Here are some basic steps you can take toward creating a functional, organized, easy-to-use pantry, no matter how big or small your space is.

1. Start by taking everything off the shelves.
2. Throw out any food that has gone bad or has passed its freshness date.

3. Wipe off the shelves and replace shelf paper if desired.
4. As you put things back in, group items by similarity and frequency of use.
5. Use the hardest-to-reach shelves for things you rarely use.
6. Place the items you frequently use where they are most visible and easily reached. I recommend eye level, if your space allows.
7. Use baskets for smaller items like seasonings or soup envelopes, ramen, pancake mixes, rice, and pasta.

WHAT TO STOCK

I think we all realize that a well-stocked pantry means different things to different people—depending, in part, on how much you entertain and how many people live in your home. Keep in mind that pantry perspectives change over time as families grow and life changes. And no two pantries are alike.

Every woman's pantry will have different items depending on her tastes and favorite recipes. For example, my friend Vicky stocks her pantry with Asian condiments and different types of rice than I have. Each cook has a different plan, so you have to customize your pantry to suit your palate. After years of shopping, I created a simple list of what I needed. It made life simpler and less stressful for me.

BAKING

The baking center is probably my favorite. Who doesn't love to have every flavor of chocolate chip known to man stocked and ready?

- sugar (white, brown, powdered)
- Stevia or other natural sugar substitute
- flour (white, whole wheat, etc.)
- baking powder
- baking soda
- cream of tartar
- baking chocolate
- cocoa
- vanilla and almond extract
- chocolate chips
- yeast
- pancake mix
- baking mixes (e.g., cake, brownies, muffins)

HERBS AND SPICES

I keep all these on hand because I use them all. Buy only what you use.

- basil
- thyme
- rosemary
- garlic powder
- onion powder
- cumin
- chili powder
- paprika
- dill
- oregano
- ginger (fresh and ground)
- dried mustard
- cinnamon
- nutmeg
- curry powder
- saffron
- pepper
- salts (kosher, sea, celery, garlic)

OILS AND VINEGARS

- oil (vegetable, olive, sesame, canola)
- cooking spray
- vinegar (white, red wine, rice, apple cider, balsamic)

CANNED GOODS

tomatoes (diced and whole)
tomato paste
tomato sauce
spaghetti sauce
beans (black, pinto, kidney,
    refried, green)
enchilada sauce
green chiles
olives
mushrooms
artichoke hearts

canned veggies (corn, green
    beans, peas)
tuna
fruit (e.g., fruit cocktail,
    mandarin oranges,
    pineapple)
cherry pie filling
soups and broth
sweetened condensed milk
evaporated milk
coconut milk

CONDIMENTS

ketchup
mustard (yellow, Dijon,
    whole grain)
pickles (dill and sweet)
mayonnaise
peanut butter
jams and jellies
honey
salad dressings
Worcestershire sauce

Tabasco
salsa
soy sauce
barbecue sauce
marinades
onion soup mix
stir-fry sauces
chutneys
Thai chilie sauces

GRAINS

rice (brown, white, wild)
pasta (lasagna, spaghetti,
    fettuccine, linguine)
oats

breads (freeze if not used
    right away)
cereals
tortillas

PRODUCE

Your supply of fresh fruit and vegetables will vary depending on the season and where you live, but these are some basics that can be kept on hand year-round.

potatoes (russet, red, sweet)
onions (white, red, green)
lettuce
peppers

avocado
garlic bulbs
lemons

REFRIGERATED FOODS

milk
eggs
butter
sour cream
half-and-half
whipping cream
buttermilk

fresh salsa
cheeses (several varieties—
    whatever you use)
deli meats
crescent rolls or biscuits
hummus

FROZEN FOODS

In addition to stocking these basics, consider freezing locally grown produce if you have the freezer space. It can be even easier than canning, and basic instructions can easily be found online or in a cookbook like *Betty Crocker*.

ground beef
ground turkey
chicken
pork
tilapia
pot roast
sausage links
peas

carrots
berries
nuts (pecans, almonds,
    walnuts, pine nuts)
frozen chicken stock
ice cream
pizza
cheese

HOME-CANNED FOODS

I realize not everyone has the time or desire to can, but for those who are interested, it can be an economical way to enjoy seasonal fruits and veggies year-round. These are some of our favorites.

pears	chutneys
peaches	salsa
applesauce	relishes
cherries	jam

Starters

Baked Brie With Chutney

This is delicious served alongside sliced Granny Smith apples or sliced pears. Place leftovers with a slice of turkey in a wrap for lunch the next day. Serves 8.

> ½ cup toasted pecan halves (or chopped)
> 8 oz. Brie cheese
> ½ cup apple-cranberry chutney

Toast the nuts ahead of time in the microwave for 1 to 2 minutes on a paper towel.

Preheat oven to 400°F. Place Brie in an ovenproof serving dish; top with the chutney and toasted nuts. Bake for 10 minutes or until the cheese inside the rind is melted. Serve with baguette slices or crackers.

Variations: Mango, peach, or apricot chutney works just as well, and walnuts, cashews, hazelnuts, or almonds can be substituted for the pecans.

Pear Bundles

The valley we live in is known for pears, so I use Bartlett pears. You can also use apples. Serves 8.

> 2 ripe pears
> 3 tsp. lemon juice
> 1 cup spinach or arugula
> 3 oz. blue cheese (use small pieces)
>   or Gorgonzola or goat cheese
> 6 oz. thinly sliced prosciutto, cut into long strips
> ¼ cup balsamic vinegar

Slice each pear into 8 wedges. Scoop out the seeds, making a shallow hole. Put the sliced pears in a shallow bowl. Pour the lemon juice on top and toss.

Place a piece of the cheese in the scooped out area of the pear, add 1 to 2 spinach leaves to the side of the pear, and roll up with a strip of prosciutto. Lay the pear bundles on a plate and drizzle the balsamic vinegar on top just before serving.

Texas Caviar Bean Dip

Inspired by my friends Kristi and Kelly, this dip is a crowd pleaser every time! Serves 10.

2 (15 oz.) cans black beans, rinsed and drained
2 (15 oz.) cans pinto beans, rinsed and drained
2 (15 oz.) cans white corn, rinsed and drained
1 (4 oz.) can chopped green chiles, do not drain
1 jalapeño chile pepper, seeded and finely chopped
    (optional)
1 red bell pepper, cored, seeded, and finely chopped
1 green bell pepper, cored, seeded, and finely chopped
1 small red onion, finely chopped
2 to 3 stalks celery, finely chopped
1 bunch cilantro leaves, finely chopped
½ cup rice vinegar
½ cup olive oil
⅓ cup white sugar
½ tsp. garlic powder
¼ tsp. cumin
1 to 2 avocados (optional)

In a large bowl, mix the black beans, pinto beans, white corn, green chiles, jalapeño, red and green bell peppers, red onion, celery, and cilantro together.

To make the dressing, stir the rice vinegar, olive oil, sugar, and garlic powder together in a small saucepan. Bring to a boil, then remove from heat and cool. Pour dressing over bean mixture and toss to mix evenly.

Salads

Chinese Chicken Salad

This salad is easy to double for a large group and can be made up ahead of time for a luncheon or brunch. Serves 6 to 8.

> 5 large boneless chicken breasts, cooked (boiled or sautéed)
>   and cut into long strips
> 1 lb. bacon, fried and crumbled
> 1 head lettuce or Chinese (Napa) cabbage, shredded
> ¾ cup chopped green onion
> 1 can (8 oz.) sliced water chestnuts, drained
> 1 cup red seedless grapes, cut in half (optional)
> ⅓ cup oil
> ⅓ cup soy sauce
> 1 T. dry mustard
> 2 T. ketchup
> 2 T. honey
> lettuce leaves

Combine oil, soy sauce, dry mustard, ketchup, and honey in large bowl. Add the chicken, bacon, lettuce or cabbage, green onion, water hestnuts, and grapes; mix and serve in a platter or bowl lined with lettuce leaves.

Classic Spinach Salad With Royal French Dressing

Be prepared for your guests to ask for this dressing recipe! It was passed along by my friend Paula and is delicious on any salad. Serves 6 to 8.

Salad:
- 2 bunches of fresh spinach (or 2 bags)
- 1 can (8 oz.) sliced water chestnuts, drained
- 6 hard-cooked eggs, sliced
- 1 small red onion, sliced
- ½ cup bacon bits or ½ lb. fresh bacon, cooked and crumbled

Dressing:
- ½ cup sugar
- ¼ cup vinegar
- 1 T. lemon juice
- 2 T. ketchup
- ½ cup oil
- 1 tsp. salt
- 1 tsp. paprika
- ½ small onion, chopped (optional)

Mix spinach, water chestnuts, eggs, red onion, and bacon bits together in a large bowl. In a small bowl, combine sugar, vinegar, lemon juice, ketchup, oil, salt, paprika, and onion. Just before serving, pour dressing (sparingly) over the salad.

Pear or Orange Green Salad With Glazed Pecans

My cousin Anni's poppy seed dressing is the best! For an additional pop of color, add a few fresh raspberries on top of the greens. Serves 6.

Salad:
- 1 pkg. (10 oz.) fresh spinach or garden greens (washed and ready to eat)
- 2 large ripe Bartlett pears, cored, quartered, and sliced, or 1 can mandarin oranges, drained
- 1 cup glazed pecans (recipe below)
- ½ cup dried cranberries
- ¼ red onion, sliced
- 1 avocado, peeled and diced (optional)

Dressing:
- ⅔ cup oil
- ⅔ cup sugar
- ¼ cup cider vinegar
- ¼ cup lemon juice
- 3 T. poppy seeds
- 1 tsp. salt
- ¼ cup chopped onions

Combine salad ingredients in a large bowl. Combine dressing ingredients and mix well. Pour dressing (to taste) over salad and toss just before serving.

Glazed Pecans:
- 2 cups pecan halves
- 1 T. butter
- ¼ cup real maple syrup
- 1 tsp. vanilla
- ½ tsp. cinnamon
- salt

Preheat oven to 300°F. Spread pecans on a baking sheet and place in the oven for 8 to 10 minutes to toast. Remove from oven and set aside to cool.

In a small saucepan melt the butter and add the maple syrup, vanilla, cinnamon, and a couple dashes of salt. Stir until combined and melted. Place the cooled pecans in a large bowl; drizzle the syrup mixture over the pecans. Toss to combine.

Spray a baking sheet with nonstick cooking spray and spread the pecans on the sheet. Return to oven for 20 to 25 minutes. When done, remove the pecans from the oven and spread them out on parchment paper so they don't stick together. Cool and enjoy!

Options: If you're short on time, any toasted nuts or store-bought glazed walnuts can be substituted for the glazed pecans. And Annie's Naturals Balsamic Vinaigrette can stand in for the poppy seed dressing.

Build Your Own Salad

A great salad doesn't have to come from a specific recipe. There are no rules—any combination of these ingredients will be delicious!

Greens
spinach
leaf lettuce
Romaine
cabbage
pasta

Nuts
pecans
walnuts
pistachio nuts
cashews

Cheese
feta
goat
Dubliner
Parmesan
Gouda

Veggies
onion
avocado
red cabbage
tomatoes
mushrooms

Meat
ham
turkey
bacon
chicken
salmon

Fruit
any berry
dried figs, raisins,
    dried
cranberries
grapes
mandarin oranges
apples

Pick one item from each category. Toss together and serve with your favorite salad dressing.

Variation: Feel free to experiment. Try doubling up on some categories and/or leaving out one or more categories altogether to find your own favorite combination.

Tip: If you're running low on salad dressing, stretch it by adding oil and vinegar.

Breads

Best Strawberry Bread

Makes 6 small loaves or 2 large loaves.

3 cups all-purpose flour
1 tsp. baking soda
1 tsp. salt
1 tsp. ground cinnamon
1 tsp. vanilla
2 cups sugar
4 eggs, beaten
1 cup cooking oil
2½ cups sliced strawberries

Preheat oven to 350°F. Spray loaf pans lightly with nonstick cooking spray. Combine all ingredients except the berries in a bowl and mix together with a wooden spoon. Stir in the berries last.

Place batter in loaf pans. Bake 35 to 45 minutes for small loaf pans, or about 60 minutes for large loaf pans.

Tip: Each oven bakes differently, so under-set your timer so that you do not overbake the bread. Cool 10 to 15 minutes before removing from pans.

Variation: Instead of strawberries, use any fresh berry.

Gift idea: This bread can also be baked in a canning jar and given as a gift—right in the jar! Use wide-mouth pint-sized jars, and wipe the inside of the jars with vegetable shortening (nonstick spray will not work). Fill jars two-thirds full and bake at 350°F 45 to 50 minutes. Makes 5 jar loaves.

Easy Cinnamon Bites With Maple Drizzle

This was a Sunday-morning treat my mom served almost every weekend! Serves 6 to 8.

    3 pkgs. (7.5 oz.) refrigerated biscuits
    ¼ cup butter
    2 T. sugar and ¼ tsp. cinnamon, mixed together
    1 cup powdered sugar
    2 T. milk
    1 tsp. maple extract

Preheat oven to 450°F. Melt butter in a 9" x 13" pan.

With a kitchen scissors, cut each biscuit into 3 pieces and place evenly in pan. Sprinkle with cinnamon and sugar. Bake 10 to 12 minutes.

Mix the powdered sugar, milk, and maple extract together. Drizzle over the top of the biscuit bites while they're still warm.

Variation: Add raisins, dried cranberries, or chopped nuts.

Easy-Stir Banana Bread

Taken from my mom's church cookbook, these loaves are easy to keep in the freezer, always ready to be given away! Makes 1 standard loaf or 4 small loaves.

    ½ cup butter, softened
    ¾ cup sugar
    2 eggs
    4 ripe bananas, mashed (enough for 2 cups)
    2 cups flour
    1 tsp. baking soda
    1 tsp. baking powder
    1 tsp. salt
    1 tsp. vanilla
    1 cup chopped nuts

Preheat oven to 350°F. Spray loaf pan with nonstick cooking spray.

Mix all ingredients together and stir with a wooden spoon. Pour into the loaf pan. Bake 50 minutes or until done.

Variation: This is another bread you can make in a canning jar. Follow the same instructions included with Best Strawberry Bread, and bake at 350°F for 45 to 50 minutes. Makes 3 jar loaves.

Main Courses

Angel Hair Shrimp Scampi

My Auntie Ellen shared this quick and easy recipe for last-minute company. Look in the freezer section of your grocery store for shrimp scampi. Serves 4.

  8 oz. angel hair pasta or spaghetti
  1 lb. frozen shrimp scampi, thawed
  1 bag (8 oz.) fresh baby spinach
  1 can (4.5 oz.) diced tomatoes, drained
  ½ cup fresh grated Parmesan cheese

Cook the pasta according to the package directions. Drain and return it to the pot to stay warm.

Cook the shrimp in a large skillet for about 6 minutes. Add the spinach and tomatoes to the shrimp mixture. Cook for an additional 5 minutes or until the spinach wilts and the shrimp turns pink.

Toss the pasta with the shrimp mixture. Sprinkle with Parmesan cheese. Serve immediately.

Chicken Chili

This chili recipe tastes even better when it sits overnight and is served the next day. Double or triple the recipe for a larger crowd. Our family's favorite is to use mango peach salsa. Serves 8 to 10.

    1 roasted chicken, pulled and cut into small pieces
    2 T. oil
    1 cup chopped onion
    1 red or yellow pepper, chopped
    6 to 8 cloves garlic, pressed
    2 (15 oz.) cans Mexican-style stewed tomatoes, undrained
    2 (15 oz.) cans pinto beans, drained
    2 (15 oz.) cans kidney beans, drained
    2 (15 oz.) cans black beans, drained
    1 to 2 cups salsa
    2 tsp. ground cumin
    2 tsp. chili powder
    1 tsp. salt

Sauté onion, pepper, and garlic in oil. Add chicken and rest of ingredients and simmer for 20 minutes, or simmer in slow cooker on low all day.

Perfect Prime Rib

This tried-and-true recipe came together by using my friend Anne's garlic/pepper coating, and then figuring out a formula to create a perfect medium-rare (130°F) piece of meat. If you follow this formula, you won't be disappointed. It works every time! Serves 12.

> 1 8-lb. prime rib (also known as rib roast), cut off the bone
> ¾ cup mayonnaise
> salt (I use sea salt)
> 12 to 15 cloves garlic, pressed
> coarse-ground black pepper

One to three days prior to serving, cover the roast with mayonnaise. Then generously season the coating with salt. Pat the pressed garlic onto the outside, and heavily cover it all with pepper. Rewrap the roast with plastic wrap and store in the refrigerator.

On the day the prime rib is to be served, let the roast sit on the counter for 3 hours before putting it in the oven.

Preheat oven to 500°F. Put roast on a roasting rack and put it in the oven for 30 minutes. Turn the oven down to 200°F and roast for 30 minutes per pound. If desired, use a meat thermometer to check the internal temperature—it should be 130°F. Remove from oven and cover with foil. Let it stand for 15 to 30 minutes before serving.

Remove the twine and set roast on a cutting board to slice. Serve with horseradish sauce.

Tip: Ask someone in the meat department to cut the meat off the bone and retie the roast for you. This will help making carving and serving easier.

Sample time schedule for an 8-lb. roast to be served at 6:30 p.m.:

10:30 a.m.	3 hours counter time
1:30 p.m.	30 minutes at 500°F
2:00 p.m.	8 lbs. x 30 minutes per lb. = 4 hours at 200°F
6:00 p.m.	Remove from oven; let stand 15 to 30 minutes
6:30 p.m.	Ready to serve!

Lemon Dill Salmon With Cucumber Sauce

Inspired by Anne, who taught me how to perfectly cook seafood, this delicious recipe can be served either hot or cold. Serves 8.

Cucumber Sauce:
- 1 cucumber
- 1 cup sour cream or plain yogurt
- ¼ cup fresh dill
- ¼ cup thinly sliced green onion
- salt to taste

Salmon:
- 1 or 2 skinless salmon fillets (2 lbs.) or 8 salmon steaks
- ¼ to ½ cup butter, melted
- ¼ cup fresh dill, chopped (or 3 T. dried)
- 1 lemon
- sea salt
- pepper (I use white pepper)

Peel the cucumber and cut lengthwise. Remove seeds, then cut into smaller sections. Place all sauce ingredients in a food processor and blend. Refrigerate for 2 hours or overnight.

To bake: Lay salmon fillets or steaks in a 9" x 13" baking dish. Squeeze fresh lemon over the salmon, then spoon the melted butter over it. Season with salt and pepper. Sprinkle with the dill. Cover dish with foil and refrigerate for about 30 minutes.

Preheat oven to 325°. Bake, covered, for about 20 minutes, until the salmon is firm. Press the back of a spatula onto the salmon to feel for firmness. Once firm, the salmon is cooked. If it feels spongy, it is not fully cooked.

To grill: Prepare low coals in a charcoal grill, or set a gas grill to low heat. Layer two 18" pieces of foil (one directly on top of the other) and fold up each side about an inch to create a rectangular "tray." Place the tray on the grill over indirect heat. Lay the salmon fillet(s) on top of the foil and cover the fish with the remaining ingredients, as described above. Cover the grill and cook 20 to 30 minutes. Do not turn the fish when grilling. Check for doneness using a spatula, as desribed above.

Serve with Cucumber Sauce on the side.

Sweet Home Spaghetti

For a sweet-savory spaghetti sauce, I recommend using Prego Traditional Italian sauce for this recipe because it has just the right flavor balance. For a healthier touch serve over spaghetti squash or zucchini noodles (see recipe on p. 55). Serves 10 to 12.

> 1 lb. ground meat (beef or turkey)
> 1 large sweet onion, chopped
> 2 T. olive oil
> 2 to 3 jars (24 oz.) Italian spaghetti sauce
> ¼ to ½ cup sugar (or 4 to 6 tsp. Stevia), to taste
> 2 lbs. dry pasta
> Parmesan cheese, freshly grated

Cook the ground meat of your choice and drain. In a separate pan, sauté chopped onion in oil. Add the cooked meat, sauce, and sugar (or Stevia). Simmer 20 to 30 minutes.

Cook pasta as directed on the package. Rinse and drain. Serve meat sauce over pasta. Sprinkle with Parmesan cheese.

Sauce tip: Double the sauce recipe and freeze half of it for another meal. You can add frozen or homemade canned tomato sauce to stretch the sauce.

Pasta tip: You can boil your pasta up to 2 days in advance. Allow it to drain thoroughly and cool, then store in resealable bags in the refrigerator. When it's time to serve, run hot water over the pasta in a colander and drain well.

Sides

Garlicky Creamy Potatoes

If you make this the day before your dinner party, it's easy to reheat and serve—and it has a more garlicky flavor. Serves 6 to 8.

    4½ lbs. potatoes
    2 cups whole milk
    2 cups heavy cream
    2 sweet onions, peeled and sliced
    6 to 8 cloves garlic, minced
    1 T. salt
    ¼ cup butter

Preheat oven to 500°F. Peel potatoes and cut in half-inch slices. Put in a large kettle with milk, cream, onion, minced garlic, and salt. Bring to a boil and simmer about 30 minutes or until tender (they should not be mushy).

Spray a large (9" x 13") roasting pan with nonstick cooking spray. Pour the potato mixture into it. Dot the top with butter and bake for 15 minutes or until bubbly and browned on top. Remove and let stand for 10 to 20 minutes before serving. Use a scoop for serving.

Variation: Prepare the potatoes the night before. The next day, bake uncovered at 350°F for 1 hour.

Veggie Casserole

This easy "garden dump" recipe came from my friend Jeannie. Replace the squash with any garden vegetables you want to use up. Serves 6 to 8.

½ cup butter, plus enough to grease pan
2 large Walla Walla onions, or other sweet onions, quartered
3 medium crookneck squash
red or yellow pepper, sliced
1 cup breadcrumbs
2 cups half-and-half
3 eggs
salt and pepper
1 cup grated cheddar cheese
1 cup grated Parmesan cheese

Preheat oven to 350°F. In sauté pan over medium heat, melt butter. Sauté veggies until softened. Grease a 9" x 13" pan with butter. Line the bottom of the baking pan with breadcrumbs and place the sautéed veggies on top.

In a mixing bowl, combine the half-and-half, eggs, and salt and pepper. Pour over the veggies. Top with grated cheese. Bake uncovered for 30 minutes.

Remove from the oven, cover with a dish towel, and let stand for 15 minutes before serving.

Tasty Green Beans

I always make extra green beans and use the leftovers in a potpie the next day. Serves 4 to 6.

> 2 T. oil
> 6 shallots, peeled and thinly sliced, or 1 small sweet onion, chopped
> 4 strips bacon (optional)
> 2 medium garlic cloves, minced
> 1 lb. fresh green beans (snapped if you prefer)
> ¼ tsp. coarse salt
> ¼ tsp. fresh ground pepper

Heat oil in a large sauté pan over medium heat. Add the shallots or onion, and bacon (if desired), and cook about 5 minutes, until shallots are softened and bacon is crisp. Add garlic and cook for an additional minute.

Add the green beans, salt, and pepper, and stir well. Cover and cook for approximately 20 minutes. Serve right away.

Pesto variation: Toss the cooked beans with pesto before serving. For a unique flavor, undercook the beans slightly, then flash cook on the grill—3 minutes in a very hot pan, stirring constantly.

Sweet and sour variation: After beans are cooked, add ¼ cup white vinegar and ¼ cup sugar; toss and serve.

Tip: Replace 1 lb. fresh green beans with 3 cans of green beans, draining 2 of the cans.

Desserts

Berry Caramel Delight

This is such an easy recipe to make ahead of time. Have your caramel sauce measured in a cup and pop it in the microwave just before serving. Fresh and light! Serves 8.

    4 cups plain or vanilla yogurt
    4 cups frozen mixed berries (or ½ pint each of fresh
        raspberries, blueberries, strawberries)
    1 cup bottled caramel sauce

Spoon the yogurt into the bottom of a 9" x 13" baking dish, or separate into individual dishes (ramekins). Sprinkle the berries on top of the yogurt.

Heat the caramel sauce on low in microwave for 1 minute. Pour the sauce over the berry mixture right before you are ready to serve.

Variation: Replace the caramel sauce with Ghirardelli white chocolate sauce.

Cake in a Jar

The flavor of this recipe puts any boxed brownie or cake mix to shame. It looks so pretty in the jar and is perfect for gift giving—it's great as a hostess gift. Serves 8 to 12.

> 1¼ cups flour
> 1 tsp. baking powder
> 1 tsp. salt
> ²/₃ cup unsweetened cocoa powder
> 1½ cups white sugar
> ½ cup chopped pecans

Layer ingredients, in the above order, in a wide-mouth quart-size canning jar. Press each layer firmly in place before adding the next layer. Screw the lid firmly in place.

Include additional toppings like marshmallows, chocolate chips, or candy bar pieces in a small baggie attached to the jar.

Attach a tag with the following instructions:

Cake in a Jar

You will need: 1 cup melted butter and 3 eggs

Preheat oven to 350°F. Grease a 9" x 13" baking pan. Empty the jar of cake mix into a large mixing bowl and add the eggs and melted better. Mix thoroughly. Spread the batter into a baking pan and top with additional toppings if desired. Bake for 25 to 30 minutes. Cool completely before serving.

Cherry Crunch

This was one of my early-entertaining recipes, passed down by my sister Di. I always keep the ingredients on hand, and it turns out perfectly every time. Delicious served warm with vanilla ice cream. Serves 8 to 10.

> 2 cans (21 oz.) cherry pie filling
> 1 box white cake mix, dry
> ½ cup butter, softened
> ½ cup nuts

Preheat oven to 350°F. Lightly grease a 9" x 13" pan. Spread the cherry pie filling in the pan. Mix together the cake mix, softened butter, and nuts. Sprinkle this mixture over the cherries.

Bake 40 to 50 minutes or until brown. Serve warm with whipped cream or vanilla ice cream.

No-Peel Apple Cake

This cake will melt in your mouth! Add a dab of freshly whipped cream on top, and you will think you died and went to heaven. Thanks to Roger and Faye for all the apples they supplied to our family over the years. Serves 8 to 10.

> 4 cups chopped, unpeeled apples (half-inch pieces)
> ½ cup oil
> ½ cup applesauce
> 1¾ cups sugar, divided
> 2 eggs
> 2 cups flour
> 1 tsp. salt
> 2 tsp. cinnamon
> 2 tsp. baking soda
> ½ cup chopped pecans

Preheat oven to 350°F. Grease a 9" x 13" baking dish. Combine apples, oil, applesauce, 1½ cups sugar, eggs, flour, salt, cinnamon, and baking soda and mix well. Pour into baking dish. Sprinkle pecans and remaining sugar over the top.

Bake 50 minutes.

Banana Cream Pie

This is a great pie filling for winter, when fresh berries aren't always available. The recipe came from my sister Linda.

> 3 T. cornstarch
> 1½ cups cold water
> 1 can (14 oz.) sweetened condensed milk
> 3 egg yolks
> 2 T. butter or margarine
> 1 tsp. vanilla
> 2 medium bananas
> lemon juice
> Easy Press Crust, prebaked (recipe on p. 49)
> whipped cream

In heavy saucepan, dissolve cornstarch in water; stir in condensed milk and egg yolks. Cook over medium heat and stir until thick and bubbly. Remove from heat; add butter and vanilla. Mix well, and then cool slightly. Slice bananas; dip the slices in lemon juice and drain. Arrange slices on piecrust. Pour filling over bananas and cover. Chill 4 hours or until set.

Spread with whipped cream and garnish with more banana slices if desired.

Variation: Skip the piecrust and alternate layers of custard, banana slices, and vanilla wafer pieces in a large glass dish.

Chocolate Chip Date Brownies

I remember eating these rich, cake-like brownies at summer picnics and after floating down the Rogue River as a child. Delicious served with whipped cream or vanilla ice cream.

  1 pkg. (8 oz.) dates
  1¼ cups boiling water
  1 tsp. baking soda
  ¾ cup canola oil
  1¼ cup sugar, divided
  1½ cups flour
  2 eggs, beaten
  ¼ cup cocoa
  ¼ tsp. salt
  1 cup chocolate chips

Chop dates and place in a small bowl. Pour boiling water over the dates and stir in baking soda. Set aside to cool.

Preheat oven to 350°. Mix together the oil, 1 cup sugar, flour, eggs, cocoa, and salt. Stir in the date mixture. Pour batter into a greased 9" x 13" pan. Mix together the remaining ¼ cup sugar and the chocolate chips and sprinkle over the top of the brownie batter. Bake 25 to 30 minutes.

Breakfast

Baked Pear Vanilla French Toast

This recipe is so mouthwateringly yummy and ideal to serve for brunch. You may just want to make two! Serves 6 to 8.

 1 cup dark brown sugar
 ½ cup butter
 2 T. water
 3 fresh pears or 28 oz. canned pears, drained
 4 cups French bread, cut into small pieces
  (better to not use the crust)
 ½ cup pecans, finely chopped
 9 eggs
 2 cups milk or cream
 2 tsp. vanilla
 powdered sugar or maple syrup

Melt the brown sugar and butter in a saucepan over medium heat. Add the water and continue heating until bubbly. Remove from heat and pour into a well-greased 9" x 13" baking pan, making sure it is spread evenly. Slice the pears thinly and arrange evenly on top of the brown sugar mixture. Sprinkle the French bread pieces over the pears, then the chopped nuts. Beat eggs, milk, and vanilla together and pour evenly over the entire mixture. Cover and refrigerate overnight.

Preheat oven to 350°F. Bake uncovered for 40 minutes, or until it becomes putty and the eggs are no longer runny. Serve with powdered sugar or maple syrup.

Breakfast Casserole

This dish is perfect for overnight company. Serves 6 to 8.

> 6 eggs
> 1½ cups milk
> 1 tsp. salt
> 1 tsp. dry mustard
> 1½ cups grated cheese
> 1 T. minced onions
> 1 lb. bulk sausage or links, cooked and drained
> 6 slices bread, crusts only, cut into small pieces
> small can sliced mushrooms, drained (optional)

Grease a 9" x 13" baking dish. Beat eggs, milk, salt, and mustard together. Stir in the cheese and onions, then add sausage and bread pieces and mix well. Mix in mushrooms if desired. Pour into baking dish and cover; let set overnight in refrigerator.

Preheat oven to 350°F and bake casserole for 30 to 40 minutes or until set.

Eggs Baked in Bacon Rings

This is a perfect way to use up garden tomatoes, and it's healthy too. Serves 4.

> 6 strips turkey bacon
> 4 slices tomato, ½-inch thick
> 4 eggs
> salt and pepper to taste

Preheat oven to 325°F.

Cook bacon slightly until it begins to shrivel, about 3 minutes. Spray a muffin tin with nonstick cooking spray. Place a tomato slice in the bottom of each cup. Circle the sides of each cup with 1½ strips of bacon. Break an egg into each cup and season with salt and pepper.

Fill any empty cups of the muffin tin with warm water. Bake 20 minutes.

Acknowledgments

Of all the dishes I've prepared, my children are the sweetest of all. Abigail, Garrett, and Elliot, you've made mothering the greatest gift in life. You three are the loves of my life. This book is for you. Abby, I'm so glad I caught my words when you put the brown bananas on top of the pie instead of on the bottom. Your scrumptious pie was what really mattered.

In my growing-up years, my sisters, Di and Linda, and I have worked together, played together, sang together, and cooked together. We've celebrated together, laughed together, and mourned together. Sisters just know how to be together, and I really love my sisters.

My dad, Milt, gave me the heritage of a loving, praying family, teaching me so much, alongside Mom. When my mother left this world, another wonderful woman stepped in. Dad met Ginny, and little did we know the gift that she would be. Oh, and because of Dad, I got a brand-new beautifully designed kitchen.

Dee has known me for years and has faithfully prayed for my life, my family, and this book project from day one. She kept me organized with my recipes, and even when we thought we were going crazy after hours of work, Dee taught me that insurmountable wasn't an option.

Believing in my RE message, my friend Barb encouraged me to start my blog, Reluctant Entertainer, in 2006. Because of Barb's inspiration, perseverance, insight, help with editing, and very special friendship from afar, *The Reluctant Entertainer* came to be. Barb, thanks for the hospitality boxes full of chocolate that kept me going!

My running partners—Jenny, Kristi, and Carrie—are my Rocks of Gibraltar. In the wee morning hours, we share anything and everything that is happening in our lives and hold it tight to our hearts. Thank you! And thank you, Carrie, for throwing the RE book–celebration dinner party when I signed my contract.

I'm so fortunate to have so many girlfriends. So many have influenced my life, and a few I mention in this book. But even for the names not recorded, I'm thankful for my fabulous girlfriends through many seasons in life. A good hostess knows that entertaining is most successful (and fun) when it's a group effort. I affectionately want to thank Terri Hay, Faye Hutchings, Jeannie Matthews, Hoppi Lilien, Anne Jantzi, Pam Darnall, Cindy Suttle and Michelle Black, whom I've learned so much from. And thank you, Myrna Wulff, for sharing your pantry tips with me!

I am deeply grateful for Kyle Duncan and Julie Smith from Bethany House, who had a vision for the RE message, and for my editor, Natasha Sperling, who remained calm in all of my madness of writing this book. She supported my ideas, and I graciously learned from her. Natasha, thank you for your excellent editorial work and friendship. Melinda Schumacher did a beautiful job with the style and design. Thanks, Mel, for the hours you put into the interior layout of RE. And a big thank-you to Janet Grant for being the best agent around. I appreciate you!

I can't even think about the *Reluctant Entertainer* message without thanking my faithful readers. Since 2006, many of you have followed my blog, sharing *your* life through *your* comments. I never dreamed that I'd be sharing the RE message in book form. This book would not be without YOU. Thank you, faithful readers!

And thanks to several bloggers who have supported me in this journey. Melissa (TheInspiredRoom.net), Nester (TheNester.com), Emily (ChattingAtTheSky.com), Kimba (ASoftPlace.net), Meredith (LikeMerchantShips.org), Selena (ApronThriftGirl.com), Rhoda

(SouthernHospitalityBlog.com), Amy (SheWearsManyHats.com), Aggie (Aggies Kitchen.com), Tina (MommysKitchen.net), Laura (OrgJunkie .com), and Tsh (SimpleMom.net) have all become real-life friends. Thanks to my blog designer and friend Darcy (GraphicallyDesigning .com), and two friends who bolstered me with courage when I needed it, Donnetta (MQCorner.blogspot.com) and Anni (4TheContemplative Artist.blogspot.com). And finally, thanks to Debbie (TheHipHostess.com), who supplied me with many beautiful aprons, some of which I'm wearing in this book. Thank you, ladies, for more than you'll ever know.

Thank you, Crissy Miller, for one of the first beautiful examples of hospitality you gave me over a garlicky Italian meal.

As I draw this long list to a conclusion, I save the deepest part of my heart for last, my husband, Paul. Not only did you provide the majority of the beautiful photography in this book, but you were my encourager when I wanted to give up, as you showed me how to press on. You are my best friend and lover in life. Entertaining would not be the same without you!

I have been so blessed by the gift of people and food. And I thank you for letting me share it with you.

Praise God from whom all blessings flow....

Bibliography

Coughlin, Paul. *Unleashing Courageous Faith: The Hidden Power of a Man's Soul.* Bloomington, MN: Bethany House, 2009.

Heatherley, Joyce Landorf. *Balcony People.* Waco, TX: Word Books, 1984.

Higgs, Liz Curtis. *Embrace Grace: Welcome to the Forgiven Life.* Colorado Springs: WaterBrook, 2006.

Moore, Beth. *Get Out of That Pit: Straight Talk About God's Deliverance.* Nashville: Integrity Publishers, 2007.

Nouwen, Henri. *The Wounded Healer: Ministry in Contemporary Society.* Garden City, NY: Doubleday, 1972.

Schaeffer, Edith. *The Hidden Art of Homemaking: Creative Ideas for Enriching Everday Life.* Wheaton, IL: Tyndale House, 1972.

Swindoll, Charles R. *Dropping Your Guard: The Value of Open Relationships.* Nashville: Word Publishers, 1998.

Recipe Index